THE BOOK OF
SALADS & BARBECUES
AND SUMMER COOKING

THE BOOK OF
SALADS & BARBECUES
AND SUMMER COOKING

a Salamander book

Published by Salamander Books Limited
LONDON • NEW YORK

Published by Salamander Books Limited
129-137 York Way, London N7 9LG, United Kingdom

© Salamander Books Ltd., 1990

Reprinted 1991

Recipes and photographs on the following pages
are the copyright of Merehurst Press, and credited
as Bottom (B) or Top (T): 9 (B), 44, 123 (T), 132,
133, 134, 135, 136, 137, 138, 139, 140, 141, 142, 143

ISBN 0 86101 6106

Distributed by Hodder & Stoughton Services, P.O. Box 6,
Mill Road, Dunton Green, Sevenoaks, Kent TN13 2XX

All correspondence concerning the content of this volume
should be addressed to Salamander Books Ltd.

CREDITS

Designers: Sarah Cooper and Tim Scott

Contributing authors: Janice Murfitt, Cecilia Norman,
Lorna Rhodes, Louise Steele

Photographers: Paul Grater, Sue Jorgensen,
Jon Stewart

Typeset by: Maron Graphics Ltd., Wembley

Colour separation by: J. Film Process Ltd., Kentscan
Limited, Magnum Graphics Limited

Printed in Italy

CONTENTS

Introduction

INTRODUCTION

Summer is the season of sunny days, warm evenings and tranquil nights. The chill winds of winter fade to become gentle breezes which stir the nodding blooms of wild flowers and garden beauties. The birds return from their southern wintering grounds to fill the woods and gardens with their cheerful songs. The world seems to become a more lively, more joyful place than it had been when storms ripped across the landscape.

It is the time of year when we take to the outdoors for our recreation and leisure. Village greens echo to the thwack of willow on leather as the home cricket teams takes on local rivals. The gentle thud of tennis racket on ball is heard in many parks. Rivers come alive with motor cruisers and rowing boats.

With the warmer weather and brighter, outdoor style of living comes a new impetus in the kitchen. A whole range of exciting fruits and vegetables becomes available as the summer sun ripens the crops. The thick stews and satisfying puddings of winter begin to loose their appeal in the face of the new, lighter diet.

It is a time of great inspiration for the cook. A time to experiment, to innovate, to surprise. Equipped with the special summer ingredients and a little practical know-how it is possible to produce an endless succession of tantalising, delicious dishes which will astound and amaze.

Warm, gentle evenings are ideal for barbecues. So fast has the idea of outside charcoal grills caught on that few households cannot boast a barbecue and a collection of implements. With a little ingenuity a barbecue can be lifted out of the usual run of sausages and chops to become a tempting and delicious feast. A few simple marinades can transform steaks and chops while various sauces can be produced to suit any taste and dish. With very little effort the spontaneous barbecue can become a truly tempting feast.

Offering more scope to the imagination in food preparation is the traditional picnic. The archetypal alfresco meal may take place high on sunblown downs where the turf is springy and soft or in quiet meadows beside a lazily drifting river. A picnic may even be a great success in the back garden, especially with young children.

Wherever the picnic takes place it offers unrivalled opportunities for the production of tempting summer dishes. Sandwiches are the favourite and popular picnic fare with most people. They are also perhaps the easiest to make and offer greatest opportunities for experimentation. Fillings can be produced which include a vast range of ingredients. Savoury anchovies, cheese and herbs can be blended together with mayonnaise or creams to form tasty moist fillings while the simple slice of ham or beef can be livened up by a dash of mustard or pickle.

Sandwiches need not take the form only of traditional filling between two slices of bread. There are open sandwiches and horn sandwiches to vary the shapes and so add increasing temptation to the spread. Indeed the various shapes can lead to fresh fillings. The horn sandwich is particularly suitable for stuffing with prawns and other small items while the sandwich roll lends itself to spreads and creamed mixes.

Salads too are favourite picnic dishes. The summer crops produce a whole host of ingredients which lend themselves particularly well to this use. The traditional salad vegetables of lettuce, tomato and cucumber can be used in conjunction with watercress, radishes and mushrooms to produce a tempting range of light snacks. It is even possible to add rose petals or dandelion leaves to green salads to give them an extra zing and excitement otherwise lacking. Dressings too can be the subject of experimentation and innovation. New combinations of standard larder ingredients can produce surprisingly exotic and tempting dressings and the addition of a more unusual herb or flavouring can lift a simple green salad from the standard to the exceptional.

But picnic salads need not be simply variations on a theme. Pasta and potatoes lend themselves to use as more filling dishes. Requiring only a small amount of preparation, pasta and potato salads provide a base on which to build the lighter, more airy dishes of an outdoor meal. Even the hungriest child can be satisfied with a healthy portion of pasta salad. The inclusion of various other tempting ingredients and a range of herbs and spices can produce satisfying salads which will decorate the spread as well as nourish the eater.

Barbecues and picnics are the fun part of any summer diet, but cannot be indulged in every day of the week. Summer cooking is as much about daily meals as is winter cooking. And the range of ingredients available in the hot months is as suitable for sound healthy eating as it is for adventurous outdoor events. The salads and sandwiches which feature so highly on picnic menus can be favourites at family lunches and suppers. Indeed they can be supplemented with a whole range of salads which are difficult to transport, bringing fresh and exciting dishes to the table.

Nor need soups be ignored during the warm weather. Cold soups can be particularly refreshing, as well as nutritious. The familiar gazpacho is only one of tempting range of cold soups which can grace any table and need only the briefest of preparation.

But perhaps the most tempting items of all in summer cooking are the vast quantities of soft fruits which ripen to perfection on hot summer days. Strawberries, raspberries and blackcurrants all have their place in desserts for picnics, barbecues or more formal meals. Perhaps at their best when served fresh with a hint of sugar and lashings of cream, the soft fruits can also be used in a wide variety of dishes. Fruit salads and open flans are tempting ways to serve such fruits while light puddings and meringues can add variety. Sharper fruits, such as gooseberries, redcurrants and blackberries are ideal for use in pies and pastries of various kinds. The blending of different fruits in cooked dishes is one of the finest arts of summer cooking, and can produce the most fascinating results.

The warm summer months offer unbounded opportunities to the adventurous cook. Opportunities for using seasonal ingredients, for new ways of presentation and for experiment which will give scope to the cook's creative talent. In this book are some of the most tempting dishes which can be produced during the hot days and evenings with a minimum of fuss and bother. There are dishes for every occasion, suggestions for experiment and exotic ingredients. Summer cuisine is perhaps the finest we have, and certainly the most enjoyable.

SOUPS

CHILLED FISH SOUP

SUMMER AVOCADO SOUP

500 g (1 lb) unpeeled cooked prawns
2 strips lemon peel
2 bay leaves
2 blades mace
salt and pepper
4 small squid, cleaned and gutted
2 spring onions, green parts only, chopped
4 tomatoes, skinned, seeded and chopped
2 tablespoons peeled and chopped cucumber

Peel prawns, putting shells, heads and tails into a saucepan. Reserve prawns. Cover with 940 ml (1½ pints/3¾ cups) water and add lemon peel, bay leaves, mace and salt and pepper.

Bring to the boil, then cover and simmer for 30 minutes. Strain stock through a muslin-lined sieve or coffee filter paper. Return stock to rinsed-out pan. Cut squid into thin rings and chop tentacles. Add to pan and cook for 5 minutes. Set aside to cool.

Stir in spring onions, tomatoes, cucumber and reserved prawns. Season if necessary. Chill for at least 1 hour before serving.

Serves 4.

2 ripe avocados
3 teaspoons lemon juice
1 clove garlic, crushed
155 ml (5 fl oz/⅔ cup) single (light) cream
625 ml (20 fl oz/2½ cups) cold chicken stock
dash Tabasco sauce
salt and pepper
½ avocado, diced, and snipped fresh chives, to garnish

Halve avocados, discard stones and scoop flesh into a blender or food processor. Add lemon juice, garlic and cream and work to a purée.

Blend in stock and season with Tabasco and salt and pepper.

Turn into a bowl, cover with plastic wrap to prevent discoloration and chill for 1 hour. Serve garnished with diced avocado and snipped chives.

Serves 4-6.

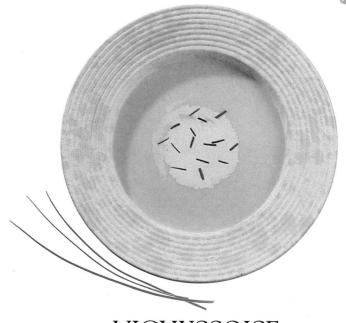

CLEAR BEETROOT SOUP

VICHYSSOISE

1 onion, coarsely grated
1 large carrot, coarsely grated
500 g (1 lb) raw beetroot, peeled and coarsely grated
parsley sprig
1 bay leaf
1 litre (1¾ pints/4 cups) chicken stock
1 egg white
juice of ½ lemon
salt and pepper
thin strips lemon peel, to garnish

Put vegetables into a saucepan with herbs and stock. Bring to the boil, then cover and simmer for 30 minutes.

Strain soup and return it to rinsed-out pan. To clear soup, bring to the boil. Whisk egg white, then pour into pan and simmer gently for 15 minutes.

Strain soup through a muslin-lined sieve into a bowl. Add lemon juice, then cool and chill. Season the soup before serving and garnish with thin strips of lemon peel.

Serves 4-6.

30 g (1 oz/6 teaspoons) butter
3 leeks, trimmed, sliced and washed
1 shallot, finely chopped
250 g (8 oz) potatoes, sliced
785 ml (1¼ pints/3 cups) light chicken stock
pinch ground mace or grated nutmeg
salt and pepper
155 ml (5 fl oz/⅔ cup) single (light) cream
snipped fresh chives, to garnish

Melt butter in a large saucepan, add leeks and shallot, then cover and cook gently for 10 minutes without browning. Add potatoes, chicken stock and mace or nutmeg.

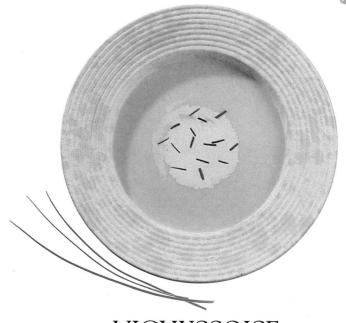

Bring to the boil, cover and simmer for 20 minutes. Purée in a blender or food processor, then pass through a sieve. Season with salt and pepper.

Set aside to cool, then stir in two-thirds of the cream. Chill until ready to serve. Ladle into bowls, swirl in remaining cream and garnish with snipped chives.

Serves 6.

CHILLED SPRING ONION SOUP

2 bunches spring onions
3 teaspoons olive oil
940 ml (1½ pints/3¾ cups) vegetable stock
salt and pepper
1 hard-boiled egg, shelled, to garnish

Trim green tops from spring onions and set aside. Chop white parts and add to a saucepan with oil, then sauté until soft.

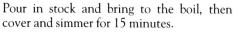

Pour in stock and bring to the boil, then cover and simmer for 15 minutes.

Chop the green parts of onions and add to soup. Cook for just 2 minutes, then set aside to cool. Chill and season with salt and pepper. Chop hard-boiled egg and sprinkle on to the soup to garnish.

Serves 4.

SOUP NORMANDE

30 g (1 oz/6 teaspoons) butter
1 Spanish onion, chopped
1 teaspoon mild curry powder
500 g (1 lb) eating apples
750 ml (24 fl oz/3 cups) chicken stock
2 egg yolks
155 ml (5 fl oz/⅔ cup) double (thick) cream
juice of ½ lemon
salt and pepper
mint leaves, to garnish

Melt butter in a large saucepan, add onion and cook gently until soft. Stir in curry powder.

Reserve 1 apple, then peel, core and chop remainder. Add to pan and cook for 1 minute. Pour in stock and bring to the boil, then cover and simmer for 20 minutes. Purée in a blender or food processor, then return to rinsed-out saucepan.

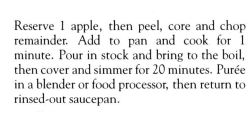

Beat egg yolks with cream and add to the soup, heating gently until thick. Do not boil. Cool, then chill for at least 2 hours. Peel, core and dice remaining apple and toss in lemon juice. Just before serving, add apple to soup, season and garnish each portion with mint leaves.

Serves 4-6.

COOL CHERRY SOUP

750 g (1½ lb) ripe black or red cherries
155 ml (5 fl oz/⅔ cup) fruity white wine
cinnamon stick
6 teaspoons sugar
grated peel and juice of 1 lemon
315 ml (10 fl oz/1¼ cups) thick sour cream
6 teaspoons brandy (optional)

Stalk and stone the cherries with a stoner, then halve them. Or, halve cherries with a knife and remove stones. Put about half the stones into a strong polythene bag and crush with a mallet.

Put the crushed stones, whole stones and stalks in a saucepan. Add wine, cinnamon stick, sugar, lemon peel and juice and 155 ml (5 fl oz/⅔ cup) water. Bring to the boil, cover and simmer for 10 minutes. Strain and return to the pan with three-quarters of the cherries and simmer for 5 minutes, until softened.

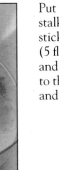

Purée in a blender or food processor. Cool, then whisk in cream, and brandy, if desired, then chill until ready to serve. Serve garnished with the reserved cherries.

Serves 4-6.

WATERCRESS & ALMOND SOUP

2 large bunches watercress
30 g (1 oz/6 teaspoons) butter
1 small onion, finely chopped
500 ml (16 fl oz/2 cups) vegetable stock
60 g (2 oz/⅓ cup) blanched almonds, toasted and
   ground
4 teaspoons cornflour
500 ml (16 fl oz/2 cups) milk
salt and pepper
flaked almonds, lightly toasted, to garnish

Wash watercress and reserve a few sprigs for garnish. Cut away any coarse stalks and chop remainder.

Melt butter in a saucepan, add onion and cook gently until soft. Add watercress and cook for 2 minutes, then stir in stock, cover and simmer for 10 minutes.

Purée in a blender or food processor and return to rinsed out pan with the ground almonds. Blend cornflour with a little of the milk, then add to pan with remaining milk and cook gently over a low heat for 5 minutes, stirring, until smooth. Remove from heat and set aside to cool. Refrigerate for at least 4 hours or overnight. Season, then serve garnished with a few toasted flaked almonds sprinkled on top and the reserved watercress sprigs.

Serves 4.

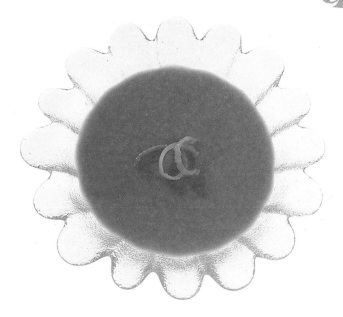

PEAR VICHYSSOISE

6 pears
juice of ½ lemon
750 ml (24 fl oz/3 cups) chicken stock
1 leek, white part only, trimmed, chopped and washed
1 potato, chopped
½ teaspoon ground ginger
90 g (3 oz/⅓ cup) low-fat fromage frais
pinch grated nutmeg
salt and pepper
1 pear and watercress sprigs, to garnish

Peel and core the 6 pears, putting fruit into a bowl of water with lemon juice.

Put pear skins and cores into a saucepan with half the stock and simmer for a few minutes to extract all the flavour. Strain into a larger pan. Drain pears, chop coarsely and put into pan with leek, potato, remaining stock and ginger. Bring to the boil, then cover and simmer for 20 minutes, until vegetables are tender.

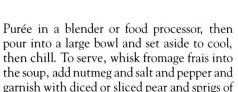

Purée in a blender or food processor, then pour into a large bowl and set aside to cool, then chill. To serve, whisk fromage frais into the soup, add nutmeg and salt and pepper and garnish with diced or sliced pear and sprigs of watercress.

Serves 4-6.

CHILLED PLUM SOUP

500 g (1 lb) red plums
155 ml (5 fl oz/⅔ cup) fruity white wine
60 g (2 oz/⅓ cup) demerara sugar
3 teaspoons lemon juice
pinch ground cloves
155 ml (5 fl oz/⅔ cup) buttermilk
½ teaspoon grated lemon peel
fine lemon peel twists, to garnish

Combine plums, wine, sugar, lemon juice, ground cloves and 500 ml (16 fl oz/2 cups) water in a saucepan. Bring to the boil, then cover and simmer gently for about 10 minutes, until tender.

Strain through a sieve and discard skin and stones from plums.

Set aside to cool, then stir in buttermilk and lemon peel. Chill the soup in freezer for 1 hour before serving. Serve icy cold, garnished with twists of lemon peel.

Serves 4-6.

CUCUMBER & YOGURT SOUP

LETTUCE SOUP

1 large cucumber
3 teaspoons olive oil
1 small onion, chopped
625 ml (20 fl oz/2 ½ cups) hot chicken stock
grated peel and juice of ½ lemon
3 teaspoons chopped fresh dill
90 ml (3 fl oz/⅓ cup) strained Greek yogurt
salt and pepper
dill sprigs, to garnish

Cut 5 cm (2 in) piece from cucumber, then chop remainder. Put oil in a pan, add onion and cook gently until soft.

Add chopped cucumber, stock, lemon peel and juice and dill. Bring to the boil, then cover and simmer for 15-20 minutes, until cucumber is tender. Purée in a blender or food processor, then turn into a bowl and cool. Stir in half the yogurt and chill.

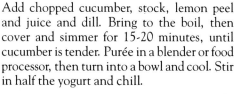

Check seasoning, then thinly slice reserved piece of cucumber. Serve the soup garnished with thin slices of cucumber floating on the surface and the remaining yogurt spooned on top with sprigs of dill.

Serves 4-6.

2 plain round lettuces
3 teaspoons oil
1 bunch spring onions, about 155 g (5 oz), chopped
1 clove garlic, crushed
500 ml (16 fl oz/2 cups) chicken stock
2 egg yolks
155 ml (5 fl oz/⅔ cup) single (light) cream
salt and pepper

Trim lettuces, discarding any damaged leaves, then separate and wash leaves. Reserve a few for garnish, then shred remaining leaves.

Heat oil in a large saucepan, add spring onions and garlic and cook until tender. Add lettuce, cover and cook until wilted. Pour in stock and bring to the boil. Then re-cover and simmer for 15 minutes. Sieve into a bowl.

Return soup to pan. Beat egg yolks and cream together and stir into soup, then cook over low heat until the soup thickens: do not boil. Cool soup, then chill. To serve, season, then roll up reserved lettuce leaves and slice finely to make a chiffonade. Stir into the soup as a garnish, then serve at once.

Serves 4.

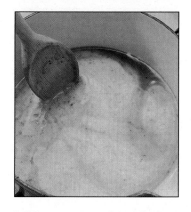

FINNISH BERRY SOUP

750 g (1½ lb) fresh or frozen mixed berries, such as
  raspberries, redcurrants, blackcurrants
250 ml (8 fl oz/1 cup) sweet white wine
cinnamon stick
60 g (2 oz/¼ cup) sugar
125 ml (4 fl oz/½ cup) whipping cream, to garnish

Select a few of the best raspberries for
garnishing and reserve. Put remaining fruit in
a pan with the wine, cinnamon stick, sugar
and 500 ml (16 fl oz/2 cups) water. Simmer for
5-10 minutes, stirring occasionally, until fruit
is soft.

Discard cinnamon stick and strain the soup
through a fine sieve.

Cool, then chill for at least 1 hour before
serving. To serve, lightly whip the cream and
swirl on to the soup, then top with the
reserved raspberries.

Serves 6.

ICED FENNEL SOUP

2 fennel bulbs, about 500 g (1 lb)
3 teaspoons sunflower oil
1 small onion, chopped
785 ml (1¼ pints/3 cups) chicken or vegetable stock
155 ml (5 fl oz/⅔ cup) thick sour cream
salt and pepper

Remove the green feathery fronds from
fennel and reserve. Roughly chop bulbs. Put
oil into a saucepan over a medium heat, add
fennel and onion, then cover and cook gently
for 10 minutes.

Add stock and bring to the boil, then reduce
heat and simmer for about 20 minutes or until
the fennel is tender.

Purée the soup in a blender or food processor.
Cool, then whisk in sour cream and season
with salt and pepper. Chill and check
seasoning again before serving, garnished
with reserved fennel fronds.

Serves 6.

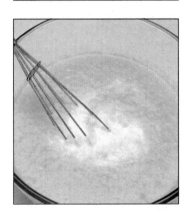

ICED MELON SOUP

SUMMER TOMATO BISQUE

2 different coloured melons, weighing about 750 g (1½ lb) each, such as galia, cantaloupe, honeydew
knob fresh root ginger, peeled
125 g (4 oz/½ cup) sugar
250 ml (8 fl oz/1 cup) dry white wine

Cut each melon in half and discard pips. Scoop out a few small balls from the green (galia) melon and set aside. Scoop out the remaining flesh from melons, keeping both varieties separate.

1 kg (2 lb) ripe tomatoes, chopped
3 spring onions, chopped
½ red pepper (capsicum), seeded and chopped
2 cloves garlic, crushed
500 ml (16 fl oz/2 cups) vegetable stock
1 teaspoon sugar
2 tablespoons chopped fresh basil
60 ml (2 fl oz/¼ cup) crème fraîche or natural yogurt
salt and pepper
1 avocado and snipped fresh chives, to garnish

Put tomatoes, spring onions, red pepper (capsicum) and garlic in a saucepan with stock and sugar.

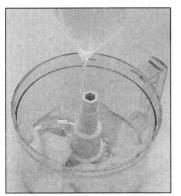

Put 625 ml (20 fl oz/2½ cups) water in a saucepan with ginger and sugar and simmer for 5 minutes. Cool, then remove ginger. Put half of the wine into a blender or food processor with one variety of melon flesh and pour in half the cooled syrup. Blend, then pour into a bowl. Repeat with remaining wine and syrup and other melon flesh.

Bring to the boil, then cover and simmer for 15 minutes. Remove from heat and leave to cool. Purée in a blender or food processor, then sieve into a bowl. Cover and chill for 2 hours. Stir in the basil, crème fraîche or yogurt and add salt and pepper.

Chill both bowls of soup for at least 1 hour. To serve, pour green-coloured soup (galia) into individual bowls, then pour orange-coloured soup (cantaloupe) in the middle. Garnish with reserved melon balls.

Serves 4-6.

Halve avocado and discard stone, peel and slice. Ladle soup into individual bowls, arrange avocado slices on top, then sprinkle with snipped chives and serve.

Serves 6.

GAZPACHO

500 g (1 lb) ripe tomatoes, skinned and chopped
½ cucumber, peeled and chopped
1 green pepper (capsicum), seeded and chopped
1 red pepper (capsicum), seeded and chopped
1 small onion, chopped
1 clove garlic, chopped
60 g (2 oz/1 cup) soft breadcrumbs
6 teaspoons olive oil
6 teaspoons red wine vinegar
500 ml (16 fl oz/2 cups) tomato juice
½ teaspoon dried marjoram
salt and pepper

Put all soup ingredients into a blender or food processor, in 2 batches if necessary.

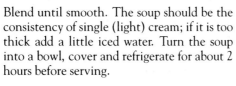

Blend until smooth. The soup should be the consistency of single (light) cream; if it is too thick add a little iced water. Turn the soup into a bowl, cover and refrigerate for about 2 hours before serving.

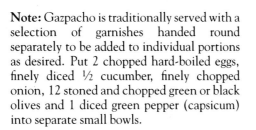

When the soup is well chilled, season if necessary and add few ice cubes.

Serves 4-6.

Note: Gazpacho is traditionally served with a selection of garnishes handed round separately to be added to individual portions as desired. Put 2 chopped hard-boiled eggs, finely diced ½ cucumber, finely chopped onion, 12 stoned and chopped green or black olives and 1 diced green pepper (capsicum) into separate small bowls.

SENEGALESE SOUP

30 g (1 oz/6 teaspoons) butter
1 small onion, chopped
2 teaspoons mild curry powder
6 teaspoons plain flour
1 litre (1¾ pints/4 cups) chicken stock
juice of ½ lemon
155 ml (5 fl oz/⅔ cup) single (light) cream or natural yogurt
125 g (4 oz) cooked skinless chicken breast (fillet), cut into thin strips
coriander leaves, to garnish

Melt butter in a saucepan, then add onion and cook gently until soft.

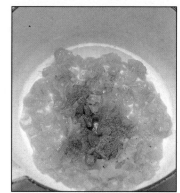

Stir in curry powder and flour and cook for 1 minute. Stir in chicken stock and bring to the boil, then simmer for 4 minutes. Strain soup through a sieve into a bowl. Set aside to cool.

Whisk in lemon juice and cream or yogurt. Stir in chicken and chill for a few hours. Serve well chilled, garnished with coriander leaves.

Serves 4-6.

Variation: Add 125 g (4 oz) peeled cooked prawns, coarsely chopped, instead of the strips of chicken.

DRESSINGS

VINAIGRETTE DRESSING

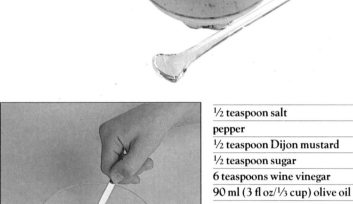

½ teaspoon salt

pepper

½ teaspoon Dijon mustard

½ teaspoon sugar

6 teaspoons wine vinegar

90 ml (3 fl oz/⅓ cup) olive oil

Put salt, pepper, mustard, sugar and vinegar into a bowl and stir together until salt and sugar have dissolved.

Pour in oil and whisk with a fork to combine well.

Alternatively, place ingredients in a screw-top jar and shake well until blended.

Makes about 125 ml (4 fl oz/½ cup).

Note: Use less oil if a sharper dressing is preferred. Use cider or herb-flavoured vinegar, or substitute lemon juice for the wine vinegar.

VARIATIONS

For Garlic Vinaigrette: Add 1 or 2 crushed cloves of garlic to the dressing.

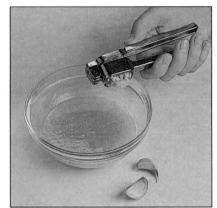

For Herb Vinaigrette: Add 1-2 tablespoons of chopped fresh herbs, such as parsley, chervil, basil, tarragon or chives, or a mixture.

For Honey Vinaigrette: Substitute 1 teaspoon clear honey for the sugar in the dressing.

For Light Vinaigrette: Replace half or all of the olive oil with sunflower oil.

MAYONNAISE

VARIATIONS

For Quicker Blender Mayonnaise: Using the same ingredients, put the egg yolk, salt and mustard into a blender. Work for 15 seconds, then add oil slowly, quickening as the mayonnaise thickens. Work in the vinegar, then season, if necessary.

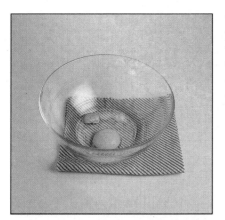

| 1 egg yolk |
| pinch salt |
| ½ teaspoon Dijon mustard |
| 155 ml (5 fl oz/⅔ cup) olive oil |
| 2 teaspoons wine vinegar or lemon juice |

Have all the ingredients at room temperature: this will help prevent curdling. Put egg yolk, salt and mustard into a bowl. Stand bowl on a damp cloth to stop it sliding about.

For Herb Mayonnaise: Add 2 tablespoons chopped fresh herbs, such as parsley, chives or tarragon, or a mixture.

Whisk ingredients together, then begin to add oil, drop by drop, whisking all the time.

For Garlic Mayonnaise (Aïoli): Add 2 crushed cloves of garlic to the egg yolk before adding the oil.

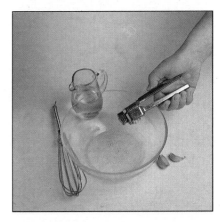

As mayonnaise thickens, add oil in a steady trickle. When all oil has been added, beat in vinegar or lemon juice. The mayonnaise can be thinned by the addition of a little hot water, if necessary.

Makes 155 ml (5 fl oz/⅔ cup).

For Light Mayonnaise: Replace either half or all the olive oil with sunflower oil, and whisk in 2 tablespoons natural yogurt.

ALMOND YOGURT DRESSING

45 g (1½ oz/⅓ cup) ground almonds
2 cloves garlic, crushed
¼ teaspoon salt
½ teaspoon black pepper
1 teaspoon grated lime peel
60 ml (2 fl oz/¼ cup) almond oil
6 teaspoons white wine
125 g (4 oz/½ cup) low fat natural yogurt
2 teaspoons chopped fresh lovage
2 teaspoons chopped fresh oregano
2 teaspoons chopped fresh parsley

Put ground almonds, garlic, salt, pepper, lime peel and almond oil in a bowl and stir together with a wooden spoon until well mixed.

Stir in wine and yogurt and beat together until blended. Cover with plastic wrap and leave in a cool place until required.

Add chopped herbs and stir well. Serve with a grated carrot and celeriac salad, mixed cooked green, broad or French beans or mixed rice and pasta salads which include meat and fish.

Makes 155 ml (5 fl oz/⅔ cup).

Variations: Replace ground almonds with ground Brazil, pine or pistachio nuts.

EGG & WALNUT DRESSING

2 hard-boiled eggs, peeled and roughly chopped
1 teaspoon light soft brown sugar
¼ teaspoon cayenne pepper
1 teaspoon Dijon mustard
1 teaspoon dry mustard
60 ml (2 fl oz/¼ cup) walnut oil
3 teaspoons cider vinegar
125 g (4 oz/½ cup) Greek yogurt
3 teaspoons chopped walnuts

Press eggs through a sieve over a bowl using a wooden spoon, or blend in a food processor.

Add sugar, cayenne pepper, mustards and oil and beat until well blended. Stir in vinegar and beat until cloudy and slightly thick. Stir in yogurt and walnuts until well mixed. Cover the dressing with plastic wrap and leave in a cool place until required.

Serve this piquant dressing with all meat and fish dishes, hot or cold. Mix together with cold rice and pasta as a base for a meat, fish or vegetable salad.

Makes 155 ml (5 fl oz/⅔ cup).

Variation: Add 4 teaspoons chopped fresh mixed herbs and replace walnut oil and walnuts with hazelnut oil and hazelnuts.

ORANGE & HERB YOGURT

1 teaspoon finely grated orange peel
6 teaspoons freshly squeezed orange juice
1 clove garlic, crushed
60 ml (2 fl oz/¼ cup) sunflower oil
125 g (4 oz/½ cup) strained Greek yogurt
2 teaspoons chopped fresh rosemary
2 teaspoons chopped fresh coriander
2 teaspoons chopped fresh parsley

Put orange peel and juice, garlic and oil in a bowl and beat with wooden spoon until well blended. Stir in yogurt.

Cover with plastic wrap and leave in a cool place until required. Stir in the chopped mixed herbs and serve at once.

Use this light dressing with sliced beetroot, chopped cucumber, potato and cooked vegetable salads and any curried dish.

Makes 155 ml (5 fl oz/⅔ cup).

Variations: Replace orange peel and juice with lime, lemon or grapefruit peel and juice, or raspberry, strawberry or currant juices.

HERBED VERMOUTH DRESSING

¼ teaspoon dry mustard
¼ teaspoon salt
½ teaspoon black pepper
½ teaspoon light soft brown sugar
140 ml (4½ fl oz/½ cup) grapeseed oil
6 teaspoons sweet red or dry white vermouth
2 teaspoons chopped fresh purple basil
1 teaspoon chopped fresh hyssop
1 teaspoon chopped fresh dill

Place mustard, salt, pepper, sugar and oil in a bowl and whisk together until well blended.

Add vermouth and whisk until cloudy and slightly thick. Cover with plastic wrap and leave in a cool place until required.

Just before using, stir in basil, hyssop and dill. Serve with a mushroom, apple, nut and celery salad, or marinate mushrooms and thin slices or chunks of melon in this dressing for 1-2 hours in a cool place, then serve as a starter.

Makes 155 ml (5 fl oz/⅔ cup).

Variations: Replace vermouth with elderflower wine and herbs with 4 teaspoons elderflower heads. Alternatively, replace vermouth with mead and substitute 1 teaspoon clear honey for the sugar. Add 3 teaspoons chopped fresh mint instead of the herbs.

TOMATO & OLIVE DRESSING

2 tomatoes, weighing about 125 g (4 oz)

¼ teaspoon salt

½ teaspoon black pepper

1 teaspoon caster sugar

125 g (4 oz/½ cup) Greek yogurt

8 black olives, chopped

3 teaspoons chopped fresh parsley

3 teaspoons chopped fresh chervil

Plunge tomatoes into boiling water for 30 seconds, then pierce skins and peel off. Halve tomatoes and remove seeds.

Press tomatoes through a sieve or place in a food processor fitted with a metal blade. Process tomatoes until puréed.

Stir in salt, pepper, sugar and yogurt until well blended. Cover with plastic wrap and leave in a cool place until required. Add olives and herbs and stir to blend well.

Serve with a celery, apple and potato salad, or a salad of cauliflower and broccoli flowerets mixed with chopped walnuts.

Makes 155 ml (5 fl oz/⅔ cup).

MINT & RASPBERRY DRESSING

6 teaspoons chopped fresh mint

3 teaspoons light soft brown sugar

140 ml (4½ fl oz/½ cup) grapeseed oil

50 g (2 oz/⅓ cup) raspberries

6 teaspoons raspberry vinegar

2 teaspoons pink peppercorns, crushed

Put mint, sugar and 3 teaspoons boiling water in a bowl and stir until sugar has dissolved. Leave to cool.

Using a wooden spoon, stir in oil until well blended. Place a sieve over the bowl and, using a wooden spoon, press raspberries through so only the seeds remain in sieve.

Add vinegar and peppercorns and beat until evenly blended. Cover with plastic wrap and leave in a cool place until required.

Serve with any mixed salad ingredients, including artichokes, avocado, lamb, chicken, duck, salmon or trout.

Makes 155 ml (5 fl oz/⅔ cup).

Variations: Replace raspberries with the same quantity of loganberries, blackberries, strawberries, redcurrants or blackcurrants.

SUNSET DRESSING

¼ teaspoon salt

½ teaspoon ground black pepper

1 teaspoon Dijon mustard

140 ml (4½ fl oz/½ cup) grapeseed oil

4 teaspoons Grenadine syrup

6 teaspoons blackcurrant wine vinegar

6 teaspoons chopped fresh basil

Put salt, pepper, mustard and oil in a bowl and whisk together until well mixed.

Add Grenadine syrup and blackcurrant vinegar and whisk until mixture has blended well together.

Stir in the basil and pour dressing into a glass serving jug or dish. Cover with plastic wrap and leave in a cool place. The dressing will separate into several layers from pale yellow to deep red with herbs suspended in the middle. Stir just before pouring.

Use to pour over mixed salads of all kinds. It is especially good with avocado and orange salad, cold meat and mixed salads or celeriac, carrot and Jerusalem artichokes.

Makes 155 ml (5 fl oz/⅔ cup).

Variation: Replace blackcurrant vinegar and chopped fresh basil with raspberry vinegar and a few fresh or frozen raspberries.

SWEET & SOUR DRESSING

1 shallot, finely chopped

1 clove garlic, crushed

¼ teaspoon salt

½ teaspoon black pepper

½ teaspoon paprika

2 teaspoons French mustard

4 teaspoons light soft brown sugar

1 teaspoon Worcestershire sauce

3 teaspoons tomato purée (paste)

140 ml (4½ fl oz/½ cup) olive oil

75 ml (2½ fl oz/⅓ cup) blackcurrant vinegar

¼ yellow pepper (capsicum)

¼ red pepper (capsicum)

Put shallot, garlic, salt, pepper, paprika, mustard, sugar, Worcestershire sauce, tomato purée (paste) and oil in a bowl. Beat with a wooden spoon until well blended.

Add vinegar and beat until cloudy and slightly thick. Cover with plastic wrap and leave in a cool place until ready to use.

Place peppers (capsicums) under a hot grill, skin side uppermost, until skin has charred and bubbled. Peel off skins and chop peppers (capsicums) finely, then set aside until cold.

Add peppers (capsicums) to dressing and stir until well blended.

Serve with mixed rice salad or a cabbage, apple and onion salad.

Makes 155 ml (5 fl oz/⅔ cup).

GRAPEFRUIT GINGER DRESSING

2 teaspoons finely grated grapefruit peel
¼ teaspoon salt
¼ teaspoon black pepper
¼ teaspoon dry mustard
140 ml (4½ fl oz/½ cup) almond oil
6 teaspoons ginger wine
6 teaspoons freshly squeezed grapefruit juice

Put grapefruit peel, salt, pepper, mustard and oil in a bowl and mix together with a wooden spoon until well blended.

Add ginger wine and grapefruit juice and beat until cloudy and slightly thick. Cover with plastic wrap and leave in a cool place until ready to use. Whisk before serving.

Serve with a red cabbage and apple salad, or beetroot and celery.

Makes 155 ml (5 fl oz/⅔ cup).

Variations: Substitute orange, lemon or lime peel and juice for the grapefruit. Add 4-5 teaspoons chopped fresh mint or rosemary to give added flavour and colour.

WALNUT DRESSING

1 teaspoon light soft brown sugar
1 teaspoon Dijon mustard
¼ teaspoon salt
½ teaspoon black pepper
140 ml (4½ fl oz/½ cup) walnut oil
6 teaspoons cider vinegar
3 teaspoons finely chopped walnuts
3 teaspoons chopped fresh sage

Put sugar, mustard, salt, pepper and walnut oil in a bowl. Whisk together until well blended.

Add cider vinegar and whisk until cloudy and slightly thick. Cover with plastic wrap and leave in a cool place until required.

Stir in walnuts and sage and serve with a mixed hot or cold pasta salad of peppers (capsicums), onions, sweetcorn and pasta.

Makes 155 ml (5 fl oz/⅔ cup).

Variations: Replace the walnut oil and walnuts with groundnut oil and finely chopped peanuts, almond oil and almonds or hazelnut oil and hazelnuts.

CELERIAC FENNEL DRESSING

CREAMY AUBERGINE DRESSING

60 g (2 oz/⅓ cup) grated celeriac
3 teaspoons chopped spring onion
6 teaspoons chopped fennel bulb
3 teaspoons chopped fennel leaves
¼ teaspoon salt
½ teaspoon black pepper
¼ teaspoon dry mustard
1 teaspoon clear honey
6 teaspoons green peppercorn vinegar
155 ml (5 fl oz/⅔ cup) thick sour cream

Put celeriac, spring onion, fennel bulb and leaves, salt, pepper, mustard and honey in a bowl and mix well together using a wooden

spoon. Stir in vinegar and sour cream, then stir until well blended.

Cover with plastic wrap and leave in a cool place until required.

Serve with cold meats and fish or with a potato and bacon salad, a mixed three-bean salad or cold pasta.

Makes about 315 ml (10 fl oz/1¼ cups).

Variations: Replace celeriac with 6 teaspoons grated fresh horseradish or extra strong horseradish sauce.

1 small aubergine (eggplant), about 315 g (10 oz)
1 clove garlic, crushed
¼ teaspoon cayenne pepper
¼ teaspoon salt
¼ teaspoon dry mustard
155 ml (5 fl oz/⅔ cup) thick sour cream
4 teaspoons chopped fresh coriander or tarragon

Place aubergine (eggplant) under a hot grill or in a preheated oven at 200C (400F/Gas 6). Cook, turning occasionally, for 15-20 minutes, until skin has charred and flesh is soft. Cool slightly, then peel off skin and place flesh in a food processor fitted with a metal blade; process until puréed. Alternatively, press aubergine (eggplant) through

a sieve using a wooden spoon.

Blend in garlic, cayenne pepper, salt, mustard and sour cream until dressing is smooth.

Cover with plastic wrap and leave in a cool place until required. Just before serving, stir in coriander or tarragon.

Use as a mayonnaise to accompany all types of salads.

Makes about 315 ml (10 fl oz/1¼ cups).

Note: This dressing can also be used as a dip with fresh sticks of vegetables. Creamy in texture, it is also good for coating new potatoes, cooked mixed vegetables, hard-boiled eggs and tuna chunks.

DILL & CUCUMBER DRESSING

5 cm (2 in) piece cucumber
¼ teaspoon salt
3 teaspoons chopped fresh dill
2 teaspoons snipped fresh chives
¼ teaspoon paprika
1 teaspoon finely grated orange peel
3 teaspoons orange juice
155 ml (5 fl oz/⅔ cup) thick sour cream

Peel cucumber, cut into 0.5 cm (¼ in) dice, then place in a bowl and sprinkle with salt. Leave for 30 minutes in a cool place.

Meanwhile, in a bowl, mix dill, chives, paprika, orange peel and juice and sour cream together. Stir until evenly blended. Cover with plastic wrap and leave in a cool place until required.

Drain cucumber, pat dry on absorbent kitchen paper, then stir into sour cream mixture.

Serve with potato salad or with cold mixed cooked vegetables such as cauliflower, beans, peas and courgettes (zucchini).

Makes about 155 ml (5 fl oz/⅔ cup).

Variation: Replace the dill with other fresh herbs, such as chopped mint, thyme or basil.

LENTIL DRESSING

60 g (2 oz/⅓ cup) red lentils
¼ teaspoon salt
½ teaspoon black pepper
¼ teaspoon grated nutmeg
3 teaspoons snipped fresh chives
155 ml (5 fl oz/⅔ cup) thick sour cream

Put lentils in a saucepan with 315 ml (10 fl oz/1¼ cups) boiling water, cover and simmer for 20 minutes, until all water has been absorbed.

Pass lentils through a fine sieve using a wooden spoon, or place in food processor fitted with a metal blade and process until puréed.

Stir in salt, pepper, nutmeg, chives and sour cream until evenly mixed, or blend in a food processor for a few seconds.

Cover with plastic wrap and leave in cool place until required. Serve with hard-boiled eggs, anchovies and olives, or with cold meats and cold cooked fish.

Makes about 155 ml (5 fl oz/⅔ cup).

Variation: For a thinner dressing, add freshly squeezed orange juice, or for a sharper flavour use vinegar.

APPLE & MADEIRA DRESSING

| 1 cooking apple, about 315 g (10 oz), peeled, cored and grated |
| 1 teaspoon light soft brown sugar |
| 90 ml (3 fl oz/⅓ cup) sunflower oil |
| 60 ml (2 fl oz/¼ cup) Madeira |

Put apple in a saucepan with 90 ml (3 fl oz/⅓ cup) water and bring to the boil; cook gently until tender.

Press apple through a sieve over a bowl using a wooden spoon, or process in a food processor fitted with a metal blade until puréed. Stir in sugar and leave mixture until cold.

Beat in oil and Madeira until well blended. Cover with plastic wrap and chill until required.

Serve with a cold pork and rice salad, mixed pasta or hot pork, poultry or game birds.

Makes 250 ml (8 fl oz/1 cup).

Variation: Add 3-4 teaspoons chopped fresh apple mint to the dressing just before serving.

CHERRY CINNAMON DRESSING

| 155 g (5 oz/1 cup) sweet cherries, stoned |
| 90 ml (3 fl oz/⅓ cup) rosé wine |
| ¼ teaspoon ground cinnamon |
| 1 teaspoon caster sugar |
| 90 ml (3 fl oz/⅓ cup) grapeseed oil |

Put cherries, wine and cinnamon in a saucepan. Bring to the boil, cover and cook very gently for 2-3 minutes, until cherries are tender.

Press cherries through a sieve into a bowl using a wooden spoon, or using a food processor fitted with a metal blade process cherries until puréed. Leave until cold.

Beat in or process sugar and oil until thick and smooth. Cover with plastic wrap and chill the dressing until required.

Serve with a cold duck, goose or pheasant salad or hot poultry or game. Mix together with apple, celery, nuts and peppers (capsicums) for a salad.

Makes about 155 ml (5 fl oz/⅔ cup).

EGG & MUSTARD DRESSING

2 hard-boiled egg yolks, sieved
1 egg yolk, raw
2 teaspoons dry mustard
6 teaspoons olive oil
1 teaspoon Worcestershire sauce
1 teaspoon white wine vinegar
2 spring onions, finely chopped
155 ml (5 fl oz/²/₃ cup) whipping cream

Put hard-boiled and raw egg yolks and mustard in a bowl and beat together with a wooden spoon.

Beat in oil drop by drop until all oil is incorporated and mixture is smooth and creamy. Stir in Worcestershire sauce, vinegar and spring onions.

Whip cream until thick, then add to egg mixture and fold in gently until mixture is well blended. Cover with plastic wrap and chill until ready to serve.

Serve as an accompaniment to cold beef, pork or chicken salads or use as a substitute for mayonnaise when making egg mayonnaise salad.

Makes 250 ml (8 fl oz/1 cup).

Variations: For Lemon Mustard Dressing: Replace vinegar with lemon juice and add 1 teaspoon finely grated lemon peel, 1 teaspoon clear honey and 3 teaspoons chopped fresh herbs. Mix in well before adding cream.

SMOKED SEAFOOD DRESSING

2 smoked trout fillets, about 125 g/4 oz, skinned
2 teaspoons finely grated lime peel
6 teaspoons freshly squeezed lime juice
155 ml (5 fl oz/²/₃ cup) single (light) cream
3 teaspoons snipped fresh chives
6 teaspoons chopped fresh watercress
¼ teaspoon cayenne pepper
watercress sprigs and lime wedges, to garnish

Place trout in a food processor fitted with a metal blade, add lime peel and juice and process until smooth.

Add single (light) cream and process again until well blended. Stir in chives, watercress and cayenne. Place in a serving dish and garnish with watercress and lime wedges.

Serve with any seafood salad or with grilled fish. This also makes a good accompaniment to a mixed vegetable or leaf salad

Makes 250 ml (8 fl oz/1 cup).

Variation: Replace smoked trout fillets with either smoked salmon or mackerel fillets.

APPETIZERS

CEVICHE

500 g (1 lb) fish fillets, such as plaice,
flounder, cod, lemon sole, mackerel or bass
juice of 5 limes
2 tablespoons olive oil
2 cloves garlic, finely chopped
3 tomatoes, skinned, seeded and chopped
1 green chilli, seeded and finely chopped
1 onion, finely chopped
12 green olives, stoned
2 tablespoons chopped fresh coriander
salt and pepper
½ avocado
lime slices and coriander leaves, to
garnish

Skin fish, cut into thin slices or
small chunks. Place in a glass dish
and pour over lime juice. Cover and
refrigerate for 24 hours.

Next day, heat oil, cook garlic
until coloured slightly. Remove
from heat, leave to cool, then add
tomatoes, chilli, onion, olives and
coriander. Season with salt and
pepper.

Drain fish, add to sauce, making
sure all the fish is well coated, then
cover bowl and chill.

To serve, divide fish and sauce
between 4 dishes. Peel and slice
avocado. Place a few slices on each
plate.

Garnish with lime slices and
coriander leaves.

Serves 4.

SEAFOOD IN WINE JELLY

185 g (6 oz) salmon steak, cut in half
12 queen scallops or 6 medium scallops
375 ml (12 fl oz/1½ cups) dry white wine
salt and white pepper
250 ml (8 fl oz/1 cup) fish stock, strained
3 teaspoons powdered gelatine
185 g (6 oz) peeled cooked prawns
dill sprigs
SAFFRON DRESSING:
3 teaspoons olive oil
1 shallot, chopped
pinch saffron threads
3 tablespoons double (thick) cream

Put salmon and scallops into a pan
with 155 ml (5 fl oz/⅔ cup) of the
wine. Season with salt and pepper,
then simmer for 5-6 minutes. Allow
fish to cool in cooking liquid.

Pour half the stock into bowl.
Sprinkle gelatine over and leave to
soften for 2-3 minutes. Stand bowl
in a saucepan of hot water; stir until
dissolved. Add remaining stock and
wine; spoon 3 teaspoons into six
125 ml (4 fl oz/½ cup) capacity
oval moulds. Refrigerate until set.

Lift cooled fish out of pan,
reserving cooking liquid. Cut
salmon into small pieces; slice scallops. Layer up the fish, prawns and
dill in each mould. Pour over a little
gelatine mixture as layers build up.
Refrigerate until set.

To make dressing, heat oil in a
small pan, cook shallot for 2
minutes, add cooking liquid from
fish and simmer for 5 minutes. Place
saffron threads in a bowl, then pour
over the hot fish liquid and leave to
cool.

Turn out jellies onto a serving
plate. Strain saffron mixture and
whisk in cream. Pour a little around
each jelly and serve garnished with
any remaining prawns and dill.

Serves 6.

CAESAR SALAD

90 ml (3 fl oz/⅓ cup) olive oil
2 cloves garlic, halved
4 thick slices bread
1 cos lettuce
6 anchovy fillets, chopped
30 g (1 oz/¼ cup) grated Parmesan cheese
SOFT EGG DRESSING:
1 egg
5 teaspoons lemon juice
3 tablespoons olive oil
1 teaspoon Worcestershire sauce
¼ teaspoon Dijon mustard
salt and pepper

Place oil in a bowl with garlic; allow to stand for 1 hour, then remove garlic.

Toast bread, remove crusts and cut into squares. Heat garlic-flavoured oil in a frying pan. Add bread cubes and fry until crisp and golden, turning frequently. Lift out croûtons and drain on absorbent kitchen paper.

To assemble salad, tear most of the lettuce into large pieces, reserving a few small inner leaves whole. Arrange whole leaves around edge of a salad bowl. Put torn lettuce in the centre with croûtons, anchovies and Parmesan cheese.

To make dressing, boil egg for 1 minute. Crack open into a bowl, scraping out from the shell. Add remaining ingredients, seasoning to taste with salt and pepper, and whisk until smooth.

Pour dressing over salad and toss gently. Serve immediately

Serves 4.

SMOKED SALMON NESTS

2 sheets filo pastry
30 g (1 oz/6 teaspoons) butter, melted
60 g (2 oz) curly endive
2.5 cm (1 in) piece cucumber
125 g (4 oz) smoked salmon
2 tablespoons Lemon Vinaigrette

Heat oven to 200C (400F/Gas 6). Cut filo pastry into twelve 8 cm (3½ in) squares. Brush with butter and place in 4 individual Yorkshire pudding tins, putting 3 pieces in each. Gently press into tins, then bake for 10 minutes until crisp and golden. Leave to cool.

Put endive into a bowl. Cut cucumber into short batons and salmon into strips. Add to bowl with dressing and toss well. Pile into pastry cases and serve at once.

Serves 4.

LEEKS À LA GREQUE

500 g (1 lb) young leeks
60 ml (2 fl oz/¼ cup) olive oil
1 onion, finely chopped
3 tomatoes, skinned, seeded and chopped
1 clove garlic, crushed
155 ml (5 fl oz/⅔ cup) dry white wine
12 coriander seeds, slightly crushed
1 bay leaf
pinch cayenne pepper
salt and pepper
2 teaspoons chopped fresh thyme
chopped black olives and thyme, to garnish

Wash and trim leeks. Cut into 5 cm (2 in) lengths, then blanch in a saucepan of boiling water for 2 minutes. Drain and set aside.

Heat 3 tablespoons oil in a large saucepan. Add onion and 1 table-spoon water and cook gently for 8 minutes. Add tomatoes, garlic, wine, coriander seeds, bay leaf and cayenne pepper. Season with salt and pepper and cook for about 15 minutes, or until tomatoes are pulpy. Add leeks and cook un-covered for 10-15 minutes until tender. If sauce is getting dry, add a little water.

Discard bay leaf, then allow mixture to cool. Transfer to a serving dish, sprinkle over thyme and chill until needed.

To serve, drizzle remaining oil over leeks and garnish with chopped olives and thyme.

Serves 4.

MARINATED MUSHROOMS

2 tablespoons olive oil
1 shallot, finely chopped
125 g (4 oz) shiitake mushrooms, stalks removed and sliced if large
90 ml (3 fl oz/⅓ cup) dry white wine
125 g (4 oz) button mushrooms, trimmed
125 g (4 oz) oyster mushrooms
1 teaspoon pink peppercorns in brine, drained
1 teaspoon green peppercorns in brine, drained
3 tablespoons walnut oil
½ teaspoon Dijon mustard
salt
1 teaspoon chopped fresh oregano
watercress sprigs, to garnish

Heat olive oil in a frying pan and cook shallot for 2 minutes. Add shiitake mushrooms, sauté for 2-3 minutes, then pour over wine and simmer for 2 minutes. Remove from heat, turn into a bowl and leave to cool.

Slice button mushrooms and halve oyster mushrooms if large. Strain the marinating liquid from shiitake mushrooms into a small bowl. Mix all the mushrooms together in a bowl with pepper-corns.

Whisk walnut oil and mustard into cooking liquid and season with salt. Pour over mushrooms and stir together. Sprinkle oregano over the top and leave to marinate for up to 1 hour before serving garnished with watercress.

Serves 4.

SMOKED FISH PLATTER

2 smoked trout fillets

2 peppered smoked mackerel fillets

3 slices bread, toasted

30 g (1 oz/6 teaspoons) butter

1 teaspoon lemon juice

100 g (3½ oz) can smoked oysters, drained

small lettuce leaves, lemon slices and parsley or dill, to garnish

HORSERADISH SAUCE:

3 tablespoons Greek strained yogurt

2 teaspoons horseradish relish

1 teaspoon lemon juice

2 teaspoons chopped fresh parsley

pepper

Skin trout and mackerel fillets and carefully cut them into small even-sized pieces. Set them aside.

Using a small fancy cutter, cut out 4 rounds from each toast. Beat butter and lemon juice together. Spread a little on the toast rounds. Place a smoked oyster on each buttered toast round.

Arrange the pieces of smoked fish and the oysters on toast on 4 plates. Garnish each plate with a few lettuce leaves, lemon slices and parsley or dill.

Make sauce by mixing ingredients together in a bowl. Spoon into a serving dish and serve with salads.

Serves 4.

JELLIED GAZPACHO SALAD

500 g (1 lb) tomatoes, skinned, seeded and chopped

1 small onion, chopped

1 clove garlic, crushed

½ teaspoon celery salt

1 teaspoon tomato purée (paste)

1 teaspoon white wine vinegar

3 teaspoons powdered gelatine

salt and pepper

TO FINISH:

7.5 cm (3 in) piece cucumber, peeled and diced

¼ Spanish onion, finely diced

½ green pepper (capsicum), seeded and diced

2 sticks celery, diced

mustard and cress, to garnish

Put tomatoes, onion, garlic, celery salt, tomato purée (paste) and vinegar into a saucepan and simmer until soft and pulpy. Sieve mixture into a measuring jug.

Sprinkle gelatine over 4 tablespoons water in a small bowl and leave to soften for 2-3 minutes. Stand bowl in a saucepan of hot water and stir until dissolved. Allow to cool, then stir into the tomato mixture, making up to 625 ml (20 fl oz/2½ cups) with water if necessary. Season with salt and pepper. Pour into 4 individual 155 ml (5 fl oz/⅔ cup) ring moulds and refrigerate until set.

To turn out, dip each mould into a bowl of hot water for a few seconds, then invert onto a serving plate.

Arrange diced vegetables around each jelly and serve garnished with mustard and cress.

Serves 4.

ITALIAN SEAFOOD SALAD

1 kg (2 lb) fresh mussels, scrubbed and debearded
500 g (1 lb) fresh clams, scrubbed
3 small squid
1 tablespoon extra virgin olive oil
185 g (6 oz) peeled cooked prawns
CAPER DRESSING:
75 ml (2½ fl oz/⅓ cup) extra virgin olive oil
2 tablespoons lemon juice
1 tablespoon chopped fresh parsley
1 clove garlic, finely chopped
1 tablespoon capers, drained
salt and pepper
parsley and lemon wedges, to garnish, if desired

Put mussels into a large saucepan with a cupful of water. Cover, cook over high heat for 5 minutes until mussles open. Remove from heat, discard any which remain closed. Allow to cool slightly.

Remove mussels from shells. Prepare clams in the same way, discarding any that remain closed.

To prepare squid, pull off tentacles and remove transparent bone in body. Remove any skin, then cut tubes into thin slices. Cut off tentacles just in front of eyes and set aside.

Heat oil in a heavy-based frying pan. Add squid rings and tentacles and sauté for about 2 minutes until opaque. Turn into a bowl and add other shellfish.

To make dressing, mix ingredients together in a bowl or screw-top jar. Pour over fish and refrigerate for 2 hours.

Serve garnished with parsley and lemon wedges, if desired.

Serves 4.

CAPONATA

2 aubergines (eggplants)
salt
125 ml (4 fl oz/½ cup) olive oil
1 small onion, chopped
4 sticks celery, chopped
440 g (14 oz) can chopped tomatoes
2-3 tablespoons red wine vinegar
1 tablespoon sugar
1 tablespoon capers, drained
12 green olives, stoned and chopped
1 tablespoon pine nuts, lightly toasted
salt and pepper
parsley sprigs, to garnish

Cut aubergines (eggplants) into small cubes, put into a colander. Sprinkle with salt and set aside to drain for 1 hour.

Meanwhile, heat 2 tablespoons oil in a saucepan, add onion and cook over medium heat for 5 minutes until soft. Add celery and continue to cook for 3 minutes. Stir in tomatoes and juice and simmer, un-covered, for 5 minutes. Add vinegar and sugar and simmer for a further 15 minutes.

Rinse aubergines (eggplants) and dry on absorbent kitchen paper. Heat remaining oil in a large frying pan and cook aubergines (egg-plants), stirring, until tender and golden. Transfer with slotted spoon to tomato sauce. Add capers, olives and pine nuts and season with salt and pepper. Continue to simmer for 2-3 minutes.

Spoon into a serving dish and cool. Serve garnished with parsley.

Serves 6.

Note: This dish tastes better if left in the refrigerator for 24 hours to allow flavours to mingle.

Variation: For a more substantial dish, garnish with flaked tuna fish.

TOMATO & MOZZARELLA SALAD

2 beefsteak tomatoes
185 g (6 oz) Mozzarella cheese, sliced
1 small purple onion, thinly sliced
salt and pepper
60 ml (2 fl oz/¼ cup) extra virgin olive oil
1 tablespoon fresh basil leaves
1 tablespoon pine nuts

Slice the tomatoes and arrange with slices of cheese, on 4 plates. Arrange onion rings on top. Season with salt and pepper, then drizzle oil over the top.

Scatter over the basil and pine nuts and serve at once.

Serves 4.

SPINACH & BACON SALAD

125 g (4 oz) young spinach leaves, washed and trimmed
60 g (2 oz) button mushrooms, sliced
3 thick slices bread, crusts removed
60 ml (2 fl oz/¼ cup) sunflower oil
1 clove garlic, crushed
185 g (6 oz) streaky bacon, rinds removed and chopped
2 tablespoons white wine vinegar
pepper

Shred spinach and put into a salad bowl with the mushrooms.

Cut bread into small squares. Heat oil in a frying pan, add bread and garlic and fry until golden. Remove with a slotted spoon and drain on absorbent kitchen paper. Wipe out pan with absorbent kitchen paper, then add bacon and cook for about 5 minutes until crisp and golden.

Pour bacon and any fat over spinach. Add vinegar to pan with a few grinds of pepper, bring to the boil, then immediately pour over salad and toss. Scatter over the croûtons and serve at once.

Serves 6.

SMOKED CHICKEN EXOTICA

3 smoked chicken breasts (fillets), skinned and boned
1 star fruit (carambola), sliced and pips removed
1 papaya, peeled, seeded and sliced
2 fresh figs, quartered
½ mango, peeled and diced
1 tablespoon chopped stem ginger, to garnish
MANGO DRESSING:
½ mango, peeled
60 ml (2 fl oz/¼ cup) sunflower oil
1 tablespoon sherry vinegar
pinch mixed spice

Slice chicken and arrange on 4 plates with slices of star fruit, papaya, figs and diced mango.

To make the dressing, put ingredients into a blender and work until smooth. Drizzle over salads or place in the centres. Garnish with ginger.

Serves 4.

CHICKEN LIVER TIÈDE

1 potato, weighing about 185 g (6 oz)
185 g (6 oz) broccoli flowerets
2 small courgettes (zucchini), sliced
250 g (8 oz) chicken livers, washed
60 ml (2 fl oz/¼ cup) virgin olive oil
salt and pepper
2 tablespoons sherry vinegar
2 shallots, thinly sliced, to garnish

Cut the potato into 0.5 cm (¼ in) matchsticks. Put into a saucepan of water, bring to the boil and cook for 3 minutes. Add broccoli and cook for 2 minutes. Add courgettes (zucchini) to pan and simmer a further 1 minute. Drain vegetables in a colander.

Cut membranes from chicken livers, then dry livers on absorbent kitchen paper. Heat oil in a frying pan, add livers and season with salt and pepper. Cook for 5 minutes, stirring constantly; they should be soft and pink inside. Remove from the pan with slotted spoon.

Divide vegetables between 4 plates, slice the livers and scatter over vegetables.

Add vinegar to pan, warm quickly, then pour over the salads. Scatter over slices of shallot and serve at once.

Serves 4 as a starter.

SOLE WITH CAPERS

2 sole fillets, each weighing about 250 g (8 oz), skinned

90 ml (3 fl oz/⅓ cup) dry white wine

2 heads chicory, chopped

1 bunch watercress, trimmed

2 teaspoons capers

MARINADE:

1 lemon

60 ml (2 fl oz/¼ cup) virgin oil

6 teaspoons lemon juice

1 tablespoon chopped fresh parsley

1 shallot, finely chopped

salt and pepper

To prepare marinade, remove peel from lemon, using a zester, and cut into shreds. Squeeze the juice from the lemon and put into a bowl with other ingredients.

Cut fish fillets in half lengthwise, then across into thin strips. Place in a frying pan with wine and poach for 2 minutes. Lift out of pan with a slotted spoon, place in marinade and leave to marinate for 10 minutes.

Arrange chicory and watercress on 4 plates. Remove fish from marinade and divide between plates.

Reduce poaching liquid to 4 tablespoons by boiling rapidly. Add capers and marinade, then warm together. Quickly pour over the salads and serve at once while the dressing is still hot.

Serves 4 as a starter.

LOBSTER & ASPARAGUS SALAD

1 cooked lobster, weighing about 750 g (1½ lb)

250 g (8 oz) fresh asparagus, cut into 5 cm (2 in) pieces

heart of 1 spring cabbage, weighing about 185 g (6 oz), shredded

tarragon sprigs, to garnish

TARRAGON DRESSING:

3 tablespoons virgin olive oil

3 teaspoons tarragon vinegar

2 teaspoons chopped fresh tarragon, if desired

salt and pepper

To prepare lobster, remove large claws and pinchers. Crack open claws; remove meat, trying to keep it in chunks. Using point of a sharp knife, split lobster into 2 pieces from head to tail. Starting at tail, remove meat, discarding brown feathery gills. Remove liver to use in another recipe. Remove dark coral if there is any and reserve. Extract meat from body with a skewer. Slice the tail meat.

Cook asparagus in a steamer for 7 minutes. Add cabbage and steam for a further 2 minutes. Arrange vegetables and lobster meat on 4 plates.

To make the dressing, mix all the ingredients in a bowl or screw-top jar, then drizzle over the salads. Garnish with lobster coral and sprigs of tarragon. Serve at once.

Serves 4 as a starter.

GOAT'S CHEESE SALAD

1 head radicchio
4 slices granary bread
two 125 g (4 oz) whole goat's cheeses
2 sticks celery, chopped
30 g (1 oz) walnut halves, chopped
celery leaves, to garnish
WALNUT GARLIC DRESSING:
3 tablespoons walnut oil
3 teaspoons red wine vinegar
1 clove garlic, crushed
salt and pepper

To make dressing, mix ingredients together in a bowl or screw-top jar.

Divide radicchio leaves and put into a bowl. Pour dressing onto the leaves and toss together, then arrange on 4 plates.

Toast bread; cut out 4 rounds. Cut each cheese in half horizontally and trim off end crusts. Place a portion of cheese on each round of toast, then place under medium-hot grill for about 3-4 minutes until golden. Transfer to plates and scatter over the chopped celery and walnuts. Garnish with celery leaves and serve at once.

Serves 4 as a starter.

PRAWNS WITH MANGE TOUT

12 raw Mediterranean (king) prawns
125 g (4 oz) mange tout (snow peas), trimmed
3 tablespoons virgin olive oil
1 tablespoon finely shredded fresh root ginger
juice and grated peel of 1 lime
3 teaspoons soy sauce

Peel prawns, leaving tail shells on. Make a small incision along spines. Remove black spinal cords from prawns. Cook mange tout (snow peas) in boiling water for 1 minute, drain and arrange on 4 plates.

Heat the oil in a large frying pan, add prawns and ginger and cook gently for 5 minutes, turning them once.

Add lime juice, peel and soy sauce; cook for 1 minute. Arrange the prawns on the mange tout (snow peas), then pour over dressing. Serve at once.

Serves 4 as a starter.

CALVES LIVER BALSAMICO

few batavia leaves
few lollo rosso leaves
60 g (2 oz) lamb's lettuce
60 ml (2 fl oz/¼ cup) extra virgin olive oil
2 large slices calves liver, weighing 250 g (8 oz), cut into ribbons
1 tablespoon shredded fresh sage leaves
2 tablespoons balsamico vinegar
salt and pepper
pine nuts, to garnish

Tear salad leaves into smaller pieces and arrange on 4 plates.

Heat oil in a frying pan, add liver and sage and cook for 2-3 minutes, stirring constantly. Remove with a slotted spoon and divide between the plates.

Pour vinegar into pan, season with salt and pepper and warm through. Spoon over the salads and serve garnished with pine nuts.

Serves 4 as a starter.

TARAMASALATA

125 g (4 oz) smoked cod's roe
125 g (4 oz/1 cup) dry breadcrumbs
2 teaspoons lemon juice
1 clove garlic, crushed
½ teaspoon black pepper
90 ml (3 fl oz/⅓ cup) olive oil
90 g (3 oz/⅓ cup) low fat soft cheese
6 black olives and parsley sprigs, to garnish

Using a sharp knife, cut through cod's roe skin and scrape out all the roe into a food processor fitted with a metal blade. Mix together breadcrumbs and 8 teaspoons cold water and add to food processor with lemon juice, garlic and pepper.

Process for several seconds until mixture is well blended. Alternatively, press cod's roe through a sieve and beat in remaining ingredients, except the garnish.

Add oil drop by drop, beating well or using food processor until all oil has been incorporated.

Beat in cheese until mixture is smooth and creamy, then spoon into a dish. Cover with plastic wrap and chill until required.

Garnish with black olives and parsley sprigs, and serve with Melba toast, biscuits or sticks of fresh vegetables.

Makes 315 ml (10 fl oz/1¼ cups).

Variation: To serve as a thinner dressing, add enough natural yogurt to make the consistency required and serve with avocados or asparagus spears.

NECTARINES & PROSCIUTTO

mixed salad leaves
2 nectarines or peaches
125 g (4 oz) prosciutto (cured ham)
fresh raspberries, to garnish, if desired
RASPBERRY VINAIGRETTE:
3 tablespoons virgin olive oil
5 teaspoons sunflower oil
3 teaspoons raspberry vinegar

Divide salad leaves between 4 plates.

Slice nectarines, halve slices of prosciutto (cured ham) and wrap around the fruit. Arrange on the salad leaves.

To make the dressing, mix ingredients together in a bowl or screw-top jar. Drizzle over the salad, then serve garnished with fresh raspberries, if desired.

Serves 4 as a starter.

AVOCADO & STRAWBERRIES

2 avocados
250 g (8 oz) strawberries, hulled
mint or strawberry leaves, to garnish
HONEY LEMON DRESSING:
2 tablespoons sunflower oil
2 teaspoons lemon juice
¼ teaspoon paprika
salt and pepper

To make the dressing, put all the ingredients in a bowl or screw-top jar and mix well. Set aside

Cut avocados in half, remove stones and peel. Dice the flesh and put into a bowl. If strawberries are large, slice or halve them, then add to avocado. Pour over dressing and toss together.

Divide between 4 dishes and serve garnished with leaves.

Serves 4 as a starter.

PRAWNS WITH GRAPEFRUIT

60 g (2 oz) young spinach leaves

1 bunch watercress, trimmed

2 ruby red grapefruit

185 g (6 oz) peeled cooked prawns

2 teaspoons chopped fresh chervil, to garnish

GRAPEFRUIT YOGURT DRESSING:

2 tablespoons Greek strained yogurt

2 tablespoons virgin olive oil

1 teaspoon clear honey

salt and pepper

Wash spinach, dry and tear leaves into smaller pieces. Mix with watercress, then divide between 4 individual serving dishes.

Cut peel and pith from grapefruit. Holding each one over a bowl to catch juice, remove segments. Arrange the segments over the salad, then scatter the prawns over the top.

To make the dressing, mix all the ingredients together in a bowl with 2 tablespoons of the reserved grapefruit juice, then spoon over the salads. Serve garnished with chervil.

Serves 4 as a starter.

MELON & TOMATO SALAD

1 small honeydew melon or 2 galia, cantaloupe or rock melons

375 g (12 oz) tomatoes, skinned

mint sprigs, to garnish

MINT DRESSING:

2 tablespoons sunflower oil

2 teaspoons sherry vinegar

1 tablespoon chopped fresh mint

pepper

Cut melon or melons in half, remove seeds, then cut the flesh into cubes (or balls using a melon scoop) and place in a bowl.

Quarter the tomatoes, remove seeds and cut each wedge across into 4 pieces. Add to the melon.

To make the dressing, mix all the ingredients together in a bowl or screw-top jar. Pour over the salad and stir gently. Cover well and chill for flavours to mingle.

Remove from refrigerator 30 minutes before serving. Spoon into 4 dishes or, if using the smaller variety of melons, spoon salad into the shells. Serve garnished with sprigs of mint.

Serves 4 as a starter.

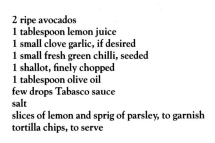

TANGY POTTED CHEESE

GUACAMOLE

125 g (4 oz/1 cup) finely grated mature Cheddar cheese
60 g (2 oz/¼ cup) butter, softened
3 teaspoons port or sherry
4 spring onions, finely chopped
½ teaspoon caraway seeds
½-1 teaspoon wholegrain mustard
¼ teaspoon Worcestershire sauce
30 g (1 oz/¼ cup) coarsely chopped walnuts
sprig of parsley, to garnish

Put grated cheese into a bowl and add softened butter. Mix well together until soft.

2 ripe avocados
1 tablespoon lemon juice
1 small clove garlic, if desired
1 small fresh green chilli, seeded
1 shallot, finely chopped
1 tablespoon olive oil
few drops Tabasco sauce
salt
slices of lemon and sprig of parsley, to garnish
tortilla chips, to serve

Cut avocados in half, remove stones and scoop flesh onto a plate. Mash well.

Stir in port or sherry, spring onions, caraway seeds, mustard and Worcestershire sauce and mix thoroughly until well combined.

Add lemon juice and garlic, if desired, and mix well. Very finely chop chilli and add to mixture together with chopped shallot.

Spoon mixture into a small dish, cover with chopped walnuts and press down lightly. Chill for at least 2 hours. Serve, garnished with parsley, with crackers or Melba toast.

Serves 4-6.

Note: This spread will keep in the refrigerator for up to 5 days.

Variation: Add 1 teaspoon chopped fresh herbs and a few pinches cayenne pepper to taste.

Stir in oil, Tabasco sauce and salt and mix well together. Turn mixture into a serving bowl, garnish with slices of lemon and sprig of parsley and serve with tortilla chips.

Serves 4-6.

BARBECUES

MARINADES AND BASTES

RICH TOMATO BASTE

1 large red pepper (capsicum), seeded and finely
   chopped
500 g (1 lb) tomatoes, skinned and chopped
1 small onion, finely chopped
1 clove garlic, finely chopped
155 ml (5 fl oz/⅔ cup) dry white wine
large rosemary sprig
2 tablespoons sunflower oil
salt and pepper

Put first six ingredients in a saucepan.
Simmer, uncovered, until thickened; purée.
Add oil and seasoning.

COGNAC MARINADE

4 tablespoons brandy
155 ml (5 fl oz/⅔ cup) dry white wine
2 tablespoons olive oil
60 g (2 oz) tiny button mushrooms, finely sliced
2 shallots, finely chopped
1 teaspoon fresh thyme leaves
4 bay leaves
1 small clove garlic, crushed
10 peppercorns, crushed
1 teaspoon salt

Combine ingredients in a lidded container.
Leave for 24 hours. Strain

SWEET & SOUR MARINADE

grated peel and juice of 1 orange
155 ml (5 fl oz/⅔ cup) clear honey
155 ml (5 fl oz/⅔ cup) red wine vinegar
3 tablespoons soy sauce
3 tablespoons Worcestershire sauce
1 tablespoon sesame oil

Combine all ingredients in a saucepan. Bring
to the boil, then simmer, uncovered, for 5
minutes until sauce reduces by about one-
third.

WARMLY-SPICED BASTE

75 g (2½ oz/¼ cup, plus 3 teaspoons) dark soft brown
   sugar
2 tablespoons red wine vinegar
¼ teaspoon ground cloves
¼ teaspoon dry mustard
1½ teaspoons ground allspice
3 teaspoons cornflour
1 small eating apple, peeled, cored and finely chopped

Place ingredients in a saucepan. Add 220 ml
(7 fl oz/⅞ cup) water. Bring to the boil,
stirring; simmer for 5 minutes or until
thickened.

FIERY CHILLI BASTE

30 g (1 oz/2 tablespoons) muscovado sugar
155 ml (5 fl oz/⅔ cup) tomato ketchup (sauce)
185 ml (6 fl oz/¾ cup) cider vinegar
2 tablespoons Worcestershire sauce
2 teaspoons chilli powder
¼ onion, finely chopped

Put sugar and 155 ml (5 fl oz/⅔ cup) water in
heavy-based saucepan. Stir until dissolved.
Add remaining ingredients; bring to boil.
Simmer until reduced by about one-third.

CITRUS SHARP MARINADE

grated peel and juice of 4 limes
grated peel and juice of 1 lemon
2 teaspoons salt
6 tablespoons sunflower oil
12 white peppercorns, bruised

Mix all ingredients together in a bowl, cover
and leave to infuse for 8 hours, or overnight.
Strain marinade before using.

Note: All the recipes given here make 315 ml
(10 fl oz/1¼ cups).

WHOLE LAURIER FLOUNDER

four 500 g (1 lb) flounder or plaice

STUFFING: 90 g (3 oz/1½ cups) soft breadcrumbs
60 g (2 oz/¼ cup) butter, melted
2 teaspoons lemon juice
1 teaspoon grated lemon peel
2 teaspoons chopped fresh parsley
salt and pepper
30 g (1 oz) cooked peeled prawns, thawed if frozen,
  finely chopped
1 egg, beaten
20 bay leaves
olive oil
16-20 vine leaves (from a packet), soaked and drained
2 lemons and parsley sprigs, to garnish

Remove heads and clean fish. Make an incision to the bone through white skin to form a pocket and lift flesh away from bone. Mix together breadcrumbs, butter, lemon juice and peel, parsley, salt and pepper to taste, prawns and egg. Spoon into pockets. Insert 3-4 bay leaves over stuffing to hold in place. Brush fish all over with oil.

Line rectangular hinged grills with oiled vine leaves. Arrange remaining bay leaves over vine leaves and place fish between. Barbecue on rack over medium coals for 10-15 minutes on each side, basting occasionally with oil, until fish is cooked. Remove fish from baskets and discard charred leaves. Serve garnished with halved crescent lemons, vandyked around edges, and sprigs of parsley.

Serves 4.

RED MULLET WITH FENNEL

four 250 g (8 oz) red mullet
fennel leaves, to garnish

MARINADE: 4 tablespoons salad oil
1 teaspoon lemon juice
1 teaspoon fennel seeds
¼ teaspoon sea salt
¼ teaspoon pepper

Mix marinade ingredients together in a large shallow dish.

Scrape away hard scales, remove gills and fins and clean inside of fish, but do not remove liver. Rinse, drain and wipe dry with absorbent kitchen paper. Score through the skin twice on each side. Put fish in marinade and leave for 1 hour, basting occasionally.

Drain fish and lay on a wire rack over hot coals and barbecue for 6-8 minutes on each side, basting occasionally with marinade to prevent sticking and encourage browning. Garnish with fennel leaves.

Serves 4.

Note: To speed up cooking an oiled tray may be inverted over fish.

LOUISIANA ANGELS

LUXURY GINGER SCAMPI

9 rashers streaky bacon, rinds removed and boned
18 button mushrooms
125 g (4 oz/½ cup) butter
2 tablespoons lemon juice
3 tablespoons chopped fresh parsley
pinch of cayenne pepper
18 fresh oysters, shelled
cornflour for dusting
6 slices crustless toast, cut into fingers

Stretch bacon rashers slightly with back of a knife. Halve rashers crosswise. Lightly fry until opaque and still limp. Drain; set aside.

750 g (1½ lb) raw Dublin Bay prawn tails (see Note)
marjoram sprigs and lemon slices, to garnish

MARINADE: 155 ml (5 fl oz/⅔ cup) salad oil
finely grated peel and juice of 1 small lemon
6 tablespoons soy sauce
1 clove garlic, crushed
1 teaspoon finely grated fresh ginger root
½ teaspoon dried marjoram

Mix together the marinade ingredients.

Cook mushrooms in saucepan of boiling water for 1 minute. Drain. To make maitre d'hôtel butter, melt butter in a pan. Remove from heat and stir in lemon juice, parsley and cayenne pepper. Keep warm. Dust oysters with cornflour. Wrap bacon rashers round oysters and alternately with mushrooms, thread onto 4-6 skewers. (Try to spear through 'eyes' of oysters to keep them in position.)

Wash prawns but leave shells intact if using unpeeled prawn tails. Mix with marinade and leave in a cool place for 2 hours. Baste occasionally.

Brush skewers generously with maitre d'hôtel butter. Barbecue on rack over medium coals for 3-5 minutes until oysters are just brown. Do not overcook or oysters will toughen and spoil. Remove from skewers and serve on toast, re-crisped on barbecue (or in the oyster shells, if desired). Spoon remaining maitre d'hôtel butter on top.

Serves 6.

Thread crosswise onto skewers and barbecue over hot coals for 7-10 minutes, turning frequently until prawn flesh is opaque. Remove from skewers and serve at once, garnished with marjoram sprigs and lemon slices.

Serves 6.

Note: Frozen, peeled raw prawn tails may be easier to obtain. These should be thawed before barbecuing.

SIMPLY-GRILLED LOBSTER

two 1 kg (2 lb) freshly cooked lobsters
125 g (4 oz/½ cup) butter, softened
2 teaspoons lemon juice
salt and pepper
lemon wedges and parsley sprigs, to garnish

On a chopping board and using a heavy sharp knife, split lobsters in half by cutting lengthwise along line down the back and through the tail. Crack claws. Remove gills, greyish sac near head and black vein which runs lengthwise along tail.

Remove the coral and beat into half quantity of butter and set aside; melt remaining butter. Sprinkle lobster flesh with lemon juice and season lightly with salt and pepper. Brush generously with melted butter.

Barbecue lobster, flesh side uppermost, on an oiled rack over medium coals for about 5-10 minutes. Turn over and cook for 3-4 minutes until lobster meat is hot and browning slightly. Serve topped with coral butter. Garnish with lemon wedges and parsley sprigs.

Serves 4.

AROMATIC GRILLED SALMON

six 185 g (6 oz) middle cut salmon
    cutlets, 2 cm (¾ in) thick
salt and pepper
flour
125 g (4 oz/½ cup) butter
a handful of winter savory or 1-2 tablespoons dried
    winter savory, moistened
6 teaspoons lumpfish caviar
winter savory or tarragon, to garnish

Rinse salmon and pat dry on absorbent kitchen paper. Season to taste with salt and pepper; dip in flour and shake off surplus.

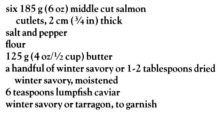

Melt butter and brush over salmon steaks. Place in a rectangular hinged basket. Sprinkle the winter savory over the coals when they are hot.

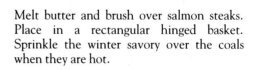

Barbecue fish on rack over hot coals for 4-5 minutes on each side, basting occasionally with melted butter. If the cutlets start to brown too quickly, reduce heat or move basket to side of barbecue. The cutlets are cooked when it is easy to move centre bone. Serve sprinkled with lumpfish caviar and garnish with winter savory or tarragon.

Serves 6.

SCALLOPS WITH TINDOORIS

SWORDFISH KEBABS

1 kg (2 lb) fresh or frozen scallops,
 thawed if frozen
12 tindooris (see Note)
155 ml (5 fl oz/²⁄₃ cup) olive oil
1 tablespoon lemon juice
1 tablespoon lime juice
¼ teaspoon lemon pepper
¼ teaspoon onion salt
lemon and lime slices, to garnish

Remove any dark veins, then rinse scallops
and pat dry with absorbent kitchen paper.
Rinse tindooris and halve lengthwise. Add to
a saucepan of fast boiling water and cook for 1
minute. Drain and leave to cool.

Combine remaining ingredients, except
garnish, in a large bowl. Put scallops into
mixture and leave for 45 minutes -1 hour,
stirring occasionally. Add tindooris during
the last 15 minutes.

1 kg (2 lb) swordfish, skinned and boned
juice of 2 lemons
2 onions, peeled
18 cherry tomatoes
155 ml (5 fl oz/²⁄₃ cup) olive oil
½ teaspoon garlic salt
½ teaspoon pepper
6-8 tablespoons finely chopped fresh chives
6-8 tablespoons finely chopped fresh parsley
lemon slices and parsley sprigs, to garnish

Cut fish into 4 cm (1½ in) cubes and
marinate in half the lemon juice for 1 hour,
turning once.

Halve onions and remove centres, leaving a
three-layer wall. Separate layers, cutting
each in half and curve to form a cone.
Alternately thread fish cubes, onion cones
and whole tomatoes onto skewers. Beat
together oil, garlic salt, pepper and remaining
lemon juice and brush over kebabs.

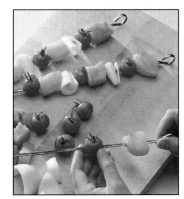

Thread scallops and tindooris onto oiled
skewers and barbecue on rack over medium
coals for 5-10 minutes, basting frequently
with marinade. Scallops are cooked when
opaque. Garnish with lemon and lime slices.

Serves 6-8.

Note: Tindooris are a vegetable the size of a
gherkin with smooth dark green skin and a
texture similar to courgettes (zucchini). They
are obtainable from most Asian stores and
supermarkets stocking exotic vegetables.

Barbecue on rack over medium coals for 10-
15 minutes, turning frequently and brushing
with oil baste. Mix together chives and
parsley and spread on a chopping board. Roll
hot kebabs in herb mixture before serving.
Serve garnished with lemon slices and
parsley.

Serves 6.

MACKEREL & RHUBARB SAUCE

6 fresh mackerel
salt and pepper
salad oil for brushing

SAUCE: 250 g (8 oz) trimmed rhubarb
1 teaspoon lemon juice
4 tablespoons sweet cider
3 tablespoons demerara sugar
¼ teaspoon grated nutmeg

Clean and gut mackerel, remove and discard heads. Season insides with salt and pepper to taste. Brush all over with oil.

Make long folded, double thickness foil strips about 1 cm (½ in) wide. Wrap around fish, placing one near the top and the other in the centre. Folding open ends twice to achieve a snug fit, at the same time form a flat loop to enable the fish to be handled easily.

Combine sauce ingredients in a heavy-based saucepan. Cover and cook gently, shaking pan occasionally until rhubarb is very soft. Purée in a blender and return to pan. Cover and keep hot. Brushing frequently with oil, barbecue the mackerel on a rack over medium coals for 7-10 minutes on each side until juices run clear when pricked deeply with a skewer. Use foil loops to help turn fish carefully. Serve with hot rhubarb sauce.

Serves 6.

PINK GRAPEFRUIT TROUT

6 small brown trout
4 pink grapefruit
60 ml (2 fl oz/ ¼ cups) dry white wine
4 spring onions, trimmed and finely sliced
16 black peppercorns, lightly crushed
2 tablespoons double (thick) cream
90 g (3 oz/⅓ cup) butter
salt

Clean and gut the fish, removing the heads, if desired. Place each fish on oiled, double thickness foil, large enough for loose wrapping.

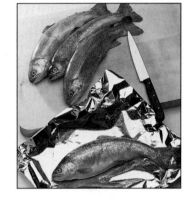

Thinly pare peel from 1 grapefruit and shred finely. Place shredded peel in a small saucepan. Cover with cold water, bring to boil, then continue cooking for 3-4 minutes to soften. Drain and set aside. Remove pith, membranes and any pips from pared grapefruit and segment flesh. Set aside for garnish. Grate peel and squeeze juice from remaining 3 grapefruit and put in a medium saucepan. Add wine, spring onions and peppercorns. Simmer for 10-15 minutes until about 155 ml (5 fl oz/⅔ cup) of liquid remains.

Remove from heat, stir in cream and butter; stir until butter melts, then strain into a jug. Season with salt to taste and mix in softened peel. Pour a little sauce over each fish and fold up foil, leaving a 2.5 cm (1 in) space over fish for steam to circulate. Barbecue on rack over hot coals for 20 minutes, but do not turn the fish packets over. To serve, open foil, pour extra sauce over trout and garnish with reserved grapefruit segments.

Serves 4.

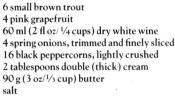

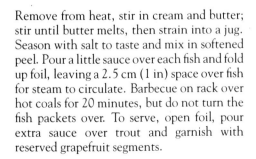

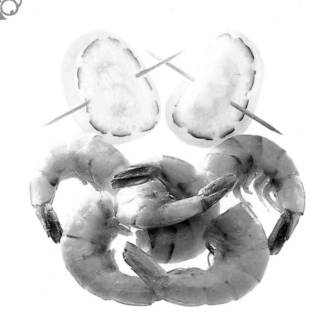

MEDITERRANEAN KING PRAWNS

juice of 1 large lemon
about 155 ml (5 fl oz/⅔ cup) salad oil
18 raw Mediterranean (king) prawns, fresh or frozen,
    thawed if frozen
2 lemons and ¼ cucumber, to garnish

To prepare the garnish remove tops and bottoms from lemons and slice middle sections thinly. Using a canelle knife, remove equidistant strips of cucumber skin lengthwise. Thinly slice cucumber. Curve cucumber slices round lemon slices before threading onto cocktail sticks.

Put lemon juice in one shallow dish and oil in another. Dip prawns, 2 or 3 at a time, into lemon juice. Shake off surplus, then dip into the oil.

Barbecue prawns on a rack over hot coals for 10-12 minutes, brushing frequently with remaining oil. Serve hot, garnished with lemon and cucumber sticks, and have finger-bowls nearby.

Serves 6.

Note: Buy whole, unpeeled king prawns for grilling. The grey-brown translucent appearance of these prawns changes to orangey-pink when cooked.

TARAMA SARDINES

6 fresh sardines
2 tablespoons lemon juice
pepper
3-4 tablespoons taramasalata
parsley sprigs, to garnish

Cut off and discard sardine heads and, using a small skewer or teaspoon, carefully clean out inside of each fish. Rinse and pat dry on absorbent kitchen paper.

Brush inside sardines with lemon juice and season to taste with black pepper. Carefully fill cavities with the taramasalata.

Place sardines in a hinged rectangular basket and barbecue over hot coals for 3-4 minutes on each side. Arrange sardines in a spoke design on a round wooden platter. Garnish by inserting sprigs of parsley into the taramasalata.

Serves 6.

Variation: Use small trout if sardines are not available and double the quantity of taramasalata.

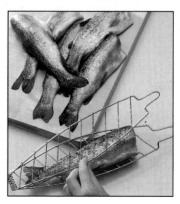

SEAFOOD KEBABS

375 g (12 oz) thick end monkfish, cut into bite-size pieces

3 plaice fillets, cut into thin strips

3 courgettes (zucchini), cut into bite-size pieces

1 small yellow pepper (capsicum), seeded and cut into bite-size pieces

12 large prawns, peeled

MARINADE:

¼ teaspoon powdered saffron

finely grated peel of 1 lime

3 teaspoons freshly squeezed lime juice

3 teaspoons clear honey

1 teaspoon green peppercorns, crushed

6 teaspoons white vermouth

90 ml (3 fl oz/⅓ cup) grapeseed oil

½ teaspoon salt

½ teaspoon black pepper

6 fresh bay leaves

3 teaspoons chopped fresh dill

GARNISH:

bay leaves

6 lime wedges

dill sprigs

To make marinade, mix all the ingredients together. Add monk-fish, plaice, courgettes (zucchini), pepper (capsicum) and prawns to marinade. Turn vegetables and fish carefully in marinade to coat evenly. Cover with plastic wrap and leave in a cool place for 1 hour. Meanwhile, soak 6 fine wooden skewers in cold water. Prepare barbecue or preheat grill.

Thread alternate pieces of each fish, with courgette (zucchini) and pepper (capsicum) in between, on to skewers with a bay leaf at the end of each. Cook for 5-8 minutes, turning only once and brushing with more marinade if necessary.

Arrange on a warmed serving dish and serve at once, garnished with fresh bay leaves, lime wedges and sprigs of dill.

Serves 6.

BARBECUED SARDINES

8 small sardines

MARINADE:

90 g (3 oz/⅓ cup) strained Greek yogurt

½ teaspoon Tabasco sauce

½ teaspoon cayenne pepper

3 teaspoons tomato purée (paste)

60 ml (2 fl oz/¼ cup) sherry

½ teaspoon salt

¼ teaspoon black pepper

1 teaspoon caster sugar

4 teaspoons chopped fresh basil

2 teaspoons snipped fresh chives

2 teaspoons finely grated lemon peel

GARNISH:

herb sprigs

chive flowers, if desired

lemon wedges

Wash and clean sardines very gently as these fish need careful handling; remove heads if desired. Dry well on kitchen paper.

To make marinade, mix yogurt, Tabasco sauce, cayenne, tomato purée (paste), sherry, salt, pepper, sugar, basil, chives and lemon peel together, stirring until evenly blended. Pour into a large shallow dish.

Add sardines 1 at a time and turn gently in marinade to coat evenly. Cover with plastic wrap and leave in a cool place for 1-2 hours.

Meanwhile, prepare barbecue or preheat grill. Arrange sardines on a fish or grill rack and cook for 5-6 minutes, turning only once, until crisp, brushing with more marinade if necessary.

Serve on a hot platter, garnished with fresh sprigs of herbs, chive flowers, if desired, and thin lemon wedges.

Serves 4.

Variation: If sardines are unavailable, use small trout or sprats.

TROUT IN SAFFRON FUMET

6 small rainbow trout
6 peppercorns
½ stick celery, coarsely chopped
1 parsley sprig
1 bay leaf
1 thyme sprig
3 thick slices carrot
1 shallot, coarsely chopped
¼ teaspoon salt
2 teaspoons white wine vinegar
125 ml (4 fl oz/½ cup) dry white wine
½ teaspoon powdered saffron
60-90 g (2-3 oz/¼-⅓ cup) butter
celery leaves, to garnish

Remove heads and tails from fish; reserve.

Taking each fish in turn, slit along belly. Open flaps and place, open-edges down, on a work surface or board. Press with thumbs along backbone to flatten. Reverse fish and lift out backbone and reserve. Put fish heads, tails and backbones in a large saucepan, add 470 ml (15 fl oz/1¼ cups) water and remaining ingredients, except butterflied fish, saffron, butter and celery leaves. Bring to boil, then remove scum. Reduce heat, cover and simmer for 30 minutes.

Strain liquor into bowl through a fine nylon sieve. Return to saucepan, add saffron and boil vigorously, uncovered, until reduced to 185 ml (6 fl oz/¾ cup). Leave to cool. Place trout, flesh-side down, in large shallow dishes. Pour saffron fumet over fish and leave to marinate for 30 minutes. Remove from marinade. Melt butter and brush over fish. Barbecue in rectangular hinged baskets over hot coals for 2-3 minutes on each side. Garnish with celery leaves.

Serves 6.

HALIBUT STEAKS WITH DILL

4-6 sprigs fresh dill weed
8 tablespoons thick mayonnaise
salt and pepper
four 2.5 cm (1 in) thick halibut steaks
4-6 tablespoons yellow cornmeal
fresh dill, to garnish

Strip the feathery leaves of dill weed away from stalk. Mix leaves with mayonnaise and season to taste with salt and pepper.

Spread both sides of each fish steak with mayonnaise, then dip in cornmeal to lightly coat.

Barbecue halibut steaks on rack over hot coals for 10-15 minutes, turning once until fish is opaque and flaky when tested with tip of sharp knife. The surface of cooked steaks should be golden brown. Sometimes browning occurs before fish is cooked through, in which case reduce heat or move to edge of barbecue to finish cooking. Garnish with fresh dill.

Serves 4-6.

DANISH PATTIES

185 g (6 oz) trimmed pork fillet
185 g (6 oz) cooked ham
185 g (6 oz) Danish salami, skinned
parsley or coriander sprigs, to garnish

DOUGH: 375 g (12 oz/3 cups) plain flour
pinch of salt
1 teaspoon baking powder
60 g (2 oz/¼ cup) white fat
155 ml (5 fl oz/⅔ cup) milk

Using a food processor or mincer, finely chop all meats together.

Sift flour, salt and baking powder into a bowl. Rub in fat finely and mix to a soft dough with milk. Divide dough into 12 balls. On a lightly floured surface, flatten each ball into a 12.5 cm (5 in) circle. Put an equal quantity of meat filling on the centre of each circle. Dampen edges and seal by drawing them together. Press well to seal. Flatten slightly with the palm of the hand.

Thoroughly grease individual pieces of double thickness foil. Place one patty, seam-side down, on each piece of foil, flattening slightly with the palm of the hand. Wrap up securely. Cook over medium coals for about 10 minutes, turning foil packets over once during cooking. To test that the filling is completely cooked, insert a sharp-tipped knife into the centre – no juices should escape. Garnish with sprigs of parsley or coriander.

Makes 12.

PITTA BURGERS

2 eggs, beaten
1 teaspoon turmeric
1 teaspoon cumin
¼ teaspoon cayenne pepper
2 cloves garlic, very finely chopped
1 kg (2 lb) freshly minced lean beef
125 g (4 oz/2 cups) fresh breadcrumbs
8 stoned green olives, chopped
6 pitta breads, halved
lettuce and stuffed green olives, sliced, to garnish

In a large bowl, beat eggs with turmeric, cumin and cayenne pepper. Stir in garlic.

Mix meat, breadcrumbs and chopped olives into the egg mixture and form into 12 burger shapes. Cook the burgers over hot coals for 8-10 minutes on each side.

When the burgers are nearly ready, warm the halved pitta breads on the side of the rack. Open the cut sides of each pitta and insert a burger. Serve wrapped in a paper napkin. Garnish with lettuce and sliced stuffed olives.

Makes 12.

BEEF & BACON SATAY

375 g (12 oz) lean beef
375 g (12 oz) unsmoked bacon rashers
1 onion, finely chopped
finely grated peel and juice of 2 lemons
4 tablespoons ground coriander
2 tablespoons ground cumin
220 g (7 oz/¾ cup) crunchy peanut butter
125 ml (4 fl oz/½ cup) groundnut oil
2 tablespoons clear honey
4 courgettes (zucchini)
spring onion tassels, to garnish

Cut beef into 2.5 cm (1 in) cubes. Put in a shallow dish. Trim bacon rashers; halve lengthwise.

Stretch bacon rashers on a work surface with a round-bladed knife drawn flat along each rasher. Roll each up tightly along its length and add to dish with the cubed beef. Mix together the onion, lemon peel and juice, coriander, cumin, peanut butter, oil and honey. Pour over beef and bacon and marinate for at least 1 hour, basting occasionally.

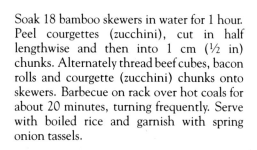

Soak 18 bamboo skewers in water for 1 hour. Peel courgettes (zucchini), cut in half lengthwise and then into 1 cm (½ in) chunks. Alternately thread beef cubes, bacon rolls and courgette (zucchini) chunks onto skewers. Barbecue on rack over hot coals for about 20 minutes, turning frequently. Serve with boiled rice and garnish with spring onion tassels.

Makes 18.

LAMB KUMQUAT KEBABS

2 large oranges
625 g (1¼ lb) lean lamb
125 g (4 oz) cooked, short-grain rice
8-10 fresh mint leaves
salt and pepper
15 kumquats, rinsed, wiped and de-stalked
olive oil for basting
mint sprigs, to garnish

SAUCE: 1 teaspoon arrowroot
¼ teaspoon sweet paprika
1 teaspoon maple syrup
2 teaspoons Cointreau

Squeeze the juice from oranges and make up to 250 ml (8 fl oz/1 cup) with water.

Pare the orange peel and snip into pieces with kitchen scissors. Cube the lamb. Using a food processor, blend the peel, lamb, rice and mint to a smooth paste; season to taste with salt and pepper. This may need to be done in 2 batches. Divide the mixture into 20 equal portions, allowing 4 portions and 3 kumquats per skewer. Mould the meat paste into lozenge-shapes around 5 skewers, interspersing with kumquats.

Barbecue the kebabs on a rack over hot coals for 10-12 minutes, turning frequently and basting with olive oil. To make the sauce, smoothly blend reserved orange juice and arrowroot together in a small saucepan. Bring to the boil, stirring continuously until sauce thickens. Stir in the paprika, maple syrup and Cointreau. Keep sauce warm and use to coat kebabs just before serving. Garnish with mint sprigs.

Serves 5.

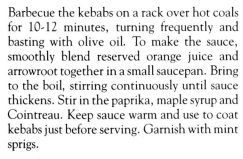

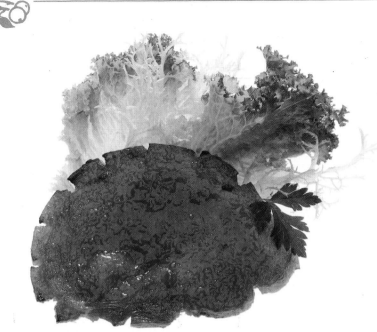

GAMMON & DAMSON SAUCE

JEWELLED PORK CHOPS

four 155 g (5 oz) gammon steaks

SAUCE: 500 g (1 lb) damsons
4 tablespoons clear honey
4 tablespoons port
4 teaspoons sunflower oil

To prepare sauce, rinse damsons and cook gently in a tightly-lidded, heavy-based saucepan until fruit is very soft and broken up. Press fruit and juice through a nylon sieve over a bowl to extract pulp and juice. Discard skin and stones.

Warm honey in a bowl over a pan of hot water and stir in the port, oil and damson pulp and juice. Leave bowl over hot water to keep honey liquified while barbecuing.

Snip edges of gammon steaks with scissors to prevent them from curling up during grilling. Coat steaks thickly with damson sauce and grill over hot coals for about 5 minutes on each side, basting frequently with sauce.

Serves 4.

Note: Reserve any remaining sauce to coat latecomer's steaks to keep them moist.

3 shallots
½ small red pepper (capsicum)
½ small green pepper (capsicum)
45 g (1½ oz) shelled pistachio nuts
6 large pork chops, 2.5 cm (1 in) thick
2 tablespoons walnut oil
2 tablespoons lemon juice
salt and pepper
12 tiny pearl onions; 3 cocktail gherkins,
    thickly sliced and 6 cherries, stoned, to garnish

Peel and roughly chop shallots. Deseed and finely dice peppers (capsicums). Halve nuts.

Put shallots, peppers (capsicums) and nuts in a bowl and cover with boiling water. Leave to stand for 10 minutes, then drain and discard liquid.

Using the tip of a sharp knife, make several small incisions into both sides of chops. Insert pieces of shallot, pepper (capsicum) and nut to stud surfaces. Mix together oil and lemon juice and use to brush over both sides of chops. Season to taste with salt and pepper. Barbecue on a rack over medium coals for 15-18 minutes on each side, basting occasionally with oil mixture. Garnish with pearl onions, gherkins and cherries, threaded onto wooden cocktail sticks.

Serves 6.

CLARET & PEPPER STEAKS

315 ml (10 fl oz/1¼ cups) claret
125 ml (4 fl oz/½ cup) olive oil
2 tablespoons green peppercorns, ground
2 tablespoons coriander seeds
eight 2.5 cm (1 in) thick sirloin steaks, trimmed
coriander sprigs, to garnish
lightly salted, whipped cream, to serve, if desired

In a large bowl, mix together the claret, olive oil, ground peppercorns and coriander seeds.

Prick the steaks deeply, then immerse them in the marinade and leave for at least 2 hours.

Barbecue the steaks on a rack over hot coals. Initially grill for 1 minute on each side to seal, then continue cooking, turning steaks occasionally and basting frequently with marinade until cooked as desired. As a general rule, a rare steak will require 3-4 minutes on each side; a medium steak 6-7 minutes and a well-done steak 8-10 minutes. Garnish with sprigs of coriander and serve plain or with a spoonful of lightly salted, whipped double (thick) cream, if desired.

Serves 8.

SOUVLAKIA

750 g (1½ lb) lean lamb
1½ tablespoons sea salt
6 tablespoons chopped fresh oregano leaves
4 tablespoons olive oil
fresh bay leaves
1 large onion, finely chopped
6-8 cherry tomatoes, halved
1 small cucumber, peeled and sliced
2 lemons, cut into wedges
315 ml (10 fl oz/1¼ cups) Greek natural yogurt
oregano sprigs, to garnish

Cut the lamb into 2.5 cm (1 in) cubes and toss in sea salt.

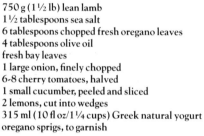

Mix 4 tablespoons chopped oregano leaves with olive oil. Skewer the lamb onto 4-5 skewers, interspersed with bay leaves. Leave generous gaps between the cubes to allow the heat to permeate more efficiently. Brush with oil mixture.

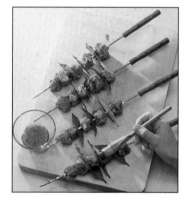

Barbecue the skewers on a rack over hot coals for 20 minutes, turning the skewers occasionally. Arrange the salad ingredients in sections on individual plates including a pool of yogurt at one side. Sprinkle with remaining oregano leaves. Remove the meat from the skewers using a fork and arrange in a line across the salad. Garnish with oregano.

Serves 4-5.

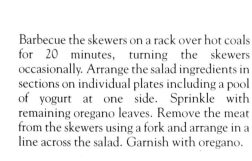

HOT DOGS WITH MUSTARD DIP

12-16 frankfurters
salt and pepper

DIP: 3 tablespoons dry mustard
250 ml (8 fl oz/1 cup) single (light) cream

To make the dip, blend the dry mustard and cream together in a bowl. Cover and leave in a cool place for 15 minutes, for the flavour to mature.

Prick the frankfurters and grill on an oiled rack over medium coals for 6-10 minutes, turning frequently. Season to taste with salt and pepper.

Wrap a twist of coloured foil round one end of each frankfurter to make it easier to hold and arrange on a platter with a bowl of dip in the centre. If preferred, cooked frankfurters can be coated with dip and inserted into long soft rolls.

Makes 12-16.

ORIENTAL SPARE RIBS

3 kg (6 lb) lean pork spare ribs
spring onion tassels, to garnish

SAUCE: 125 ml (4 fl oz/½ cup) hoisin sauce
125 ml (4 fl oz/½ cup) miso paste
315 ml (10 fl oz/1¼ cups) tomato purée (paste)
1½ teaspoons ground ginger
1½ teaspoons Chinese five-spice powder
185 g (6 oz/1 cup) muscovado sugar
3 cloves garlic, crushed
1 teaspoon salt
2 tablespoons saki (rice wine) or dry sherry

Separate the ribs and trim away most of the fat.

In a bowl, combine sauce ingredients and spread all over the ribs. Put the sauced ribs in a large shallow dish. Cover and leave in the refrigerator for at least 4 hours, or preferably overnight.

Place a drip pan in medium hot coals and barbecue ribs on a rack above the pan for 45-60 minutes, turning occasionally and basting with sauce. Heat any remaining sauce gently and serve separately. Garnish ribs with spring onion tassels.

Serves 8.

Note: Offer guests warmed damp cloths or sachets of finger wipes.

PORKIES WITH CREAMY DIP

VERMONT PORK CHOPS

8-12 low-fat, thick pork or beef sausages
oil for brushing

CREAMY DIP: 45 g (1½ oz/3 tablespoons) grated
   horseradish
60 g (2 oz/¼ cup) cream cheese
2 tablespoons lemon juice
½ teaspoon sugar
½ teaspoon salt
155 ml (5 fl oz/⅔ cup) thick sour cream

To make dip, blend horseradish, cream
cheese, lemon juice, sugar and salt together.
Gradually stir in thick sour cream. Cover and
chill until required.

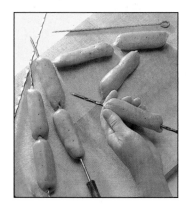

Prick sausages and thread onto skewers.
Brush with oil. Barbecue on a rack over
medium coals for 12-15 minutes until cooked
through, turning frequently.

Arrange hot sausages in a circle on a wooden
platter and place the prepared dip in the
centre. Serve with salads.

Serves 8-12.

4 pork chops, 2.5 cm (1 in) thick
8-12 shelled pecan nuts, dipped in maple syrup, and
   spring onion tassels, to garnish
MARINADE: 4 spring onions, trimmed and finely sliced
2 cloves garlic, very finely chopped
4 tablespoons maple syrup
4 teaspoons tomato ketchup (sauce)
250 ml (8 fl oz/1 cup) unsweetened apple juice
large pinch chilli powder
large pinch ground cinnamon
large pinch pepper
1 teaspoon salt

Trim any surplus fat and pierce the chops on
both sides.

Combine the marinade ingredients in a large
shallow dish, stirring briskly with a fork to
thoroughly blend in the tomato ketchup
(sauce). Add the chops, turning them over to
coat both sides. Cover and refrigerate for at
least 2 hours, turning the chops over once or
twice during this time.

Barbecue the chops on a rack over medium
coals for 15-20 minutes on each side, basting
frequently with the marinade. Just before
serving, spoon the remaining marinade over
the chops, evenly distributing any spring
onions that may still be in the bottom of the
dish. Top each chop with 2 or 3 pecans and
garnish with spring onion tassels. Serve with
roast sweet potatoes.

Serves 4.

DRUNKEN ROAST PORK

1.5 kg (3 lb) joint pork, boned and rolled
30 g (1 oz/6 teaspoons) butter
1 large onion, chopped
2 carrots, thinly sliced
2 sticks celery, finely sliced
1 large leek, washed and sliced
155 ml (5 fl oz/⅔ cup) medium red wine
1 tablespoon fresh thyme leaves
2 teaspoons fresh tarragon leaves
salt and pepper
2 tablespoons dry sherry
few thyme sprigs
2 tablespoons brandy
thyme and tarragon sprigs, to garnish

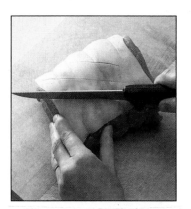

Score skin of joint; secure with string.

Place pork on a rack in a covered barbecue, and roast over low coals for about 2 hours. Unless using a spit, turn joint every 15 minutes to ensure even cooking. While roast is cooking, prepare sauce. Melt butter in a medium saucepan and gently fry onion until brown. Add carrots, celery, leek, wine and herbs. Cover and simmer, stirring occasionally, until vegetables are very soft. Pass through a sieve or purée mixture. Return to pan and season to taste with salt and pepper. Stir in sherry.

When the joint is thoroughly cooked in the centre (and registers a temperature of 75C (170F) on a meat thermometer), pierce meat in several places and insert sprigs of fresh thyme. Place on a hot flameproof serving platter. Pour brandy into a metal ladle and heat gently over barbecue for a few seconds until warm. Pour over joint and immediately ignite. Spoon brandied juice into reheated sauce. Serve joint sliced, with a little sauce to side of each portion. Garnish.

Serves 6-8.

BEEF IN TAHINI PASTE

625 g (1¼ lb) beef fillet
4 tablespoons tahini (sesame seed paste)
8 tablespoons sesame oil
½ teaspoon garlic salt
1 tablespoon lemon juice
8 spring onions, finely chopped
pepper
3 tablespoons sesame seeds, toasted
spring onion tassels, to garnish

Slice beef across the grain into 20-25 thin slices.

In a bowl, combine tahini, sesame oil, garlic salt, lemon juice and onions; season to taste with pepper. Using tongs, dip the beef slivers, one at a time, into the tahini baste, then spread them out on a board or tray. Cover with plastic wrap or foil and leave for at least 1 hour for the flavours to impregnate the meat. Reserve the tahini baste.

Prepare a hot barbecue grill and press the meat slices, basted-sides down, onto the rack. Using barbecue tongs, turn the slices over after 30 seconds and brush with the remaining baste. Grill for a further 1-1½ minutes. Arrange on a hot platter and sprinkle with toasted sesame seeds. Garnish with spring onion tassels.

Serves 6-7.

CALVES LIVER KEBABS

1 kg (2 lb) calves liver
6 tablespoons red wine
6 tablespoons sunflower oil
1 tablespoon Dijon mustard
½ teaspoon onion salt
½ teaspoon pepper
375 g (12 oz) small mushrooms
fresh herbs, to garnish, if desired

Trim the liver and cut into 4 cm (1½ in) chunks.

In a large bowl, combine wine, oil, mustard, onion salt and pepper. Add liver and mushrooms. Mix thoroughly to coat. Marinate in the refrigerator for at least 1 hour, turning occasionally.

Thread the chunks of liver and mushrooms onto skewers. Barbecue on the rack over hot coals for 10-15 minutes, turning frequently and basting with marinade. Do not overcook or liver will become dry and tough. Garnish with fresh herbs, if desired. Serve with buttered egg noodles.

Serves 6-8.

MEXICAN MUFFINS

four 90 g (3 oz) fillet steaks, 1 cm (½ in) thick
1 large or 2 small ripe but firm avocados
2 teaspoons fresh lemon juice
60 g (2 oz) Mycella cheese, crumbled
2 muffins
cayenne pepper

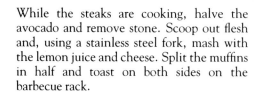

Grill the steaks on an oiled rack over hot coals according to desired doneness.

While the steaks are cooking, halve the avocado and remove stone. Scoop out flesh and, using a stainless steel fork, mash with the lemon juice and cheese. Split the muffins in half and toast on both sides on the barbecue rack.

When the steaks are cooked spread with half the avocado mixture, cover with toasted muffin halves, then invert onto hot serving plates so that the muffins form a base. Top with a dollop of remaining avocado mixture and sprinkle with cayenne pepper.

Serves 4.

Note: The avocado mixture should not be prepared in advance or it will discolour.

LAMB & LANCASHIRE SAUCE

BACON LATTICE STEAKS

375 g (12 oz) ground lamb
1 egg, beaten
1 teaspoon dried rosemary
60 g (2 oz/½ cup) fresh white breadcrumbs
1 small red pepper (capsicum), cored, seeded and
   minced
1 teaspoon Tabasco sauce
½ teaspoon onion salt
½ teaspoon pepper

SAUCE: 7 g (¼ oz/1½ teaspoons) butter
7 g (¼ oz/3 teaspoons) plain flour
125 ml (4 fl oz/½ cup) milk
1 egg yolk
75 ml (2½ fl oz/⅓ cup) thick sour cream
60 g (2 oz) Lancashire cheese, crumbled

four 235 g (7½ oz) sirloin steaks, 2.5 cm (1 in) thick
4 thin lean smoked bacon rashers
pepper
60 ml (2 fl oz/¼ cup) olive oil
185 g (6 oz) coleslaw
parsley sprigs, to garnish, if desired

Make 3 deep diagonal slashes lengthwise and
3 slashes crosswise on each side of the steaks
but do not cut right through.

Thoroughly mix the lamb, egg, rosemary,
breadcrumbs, minced pepper, Tabasco, onion
salt and pepper. Shape the mixture into about
16 rectangular fingers and refrigerate for 30
minutes. Meanwhile make the sauce. Melt
the butter in a small saucepan, stir in the
flour, remove from the heat and thoroughly
blend in the milk. Cook over moderate heat,
stirring continuously until sauce thickens to
the consistency of thin cream. Remove pan
from heat. Blend the egg yolk with the cream
and pour into pan. Mix in cheese. Cook
gently until cheese has just melted.

Cut the bacon into thin strips and insert into
the slashes to form a lattice. Press with the
palm of the hand. Season the steaks with
pepper and brush all over with oil.

Barbecue the lamb fingers on an oiled rack
over hot coals for 5-6 minutes on each side,
reducing the heat if they become too brown.
Arrange 4 neat fingers in a fan shape on each
plate and spoon some sauce over the tips,
allowing it to form a pool.

Serves 4.

Note: Garnish the lamb fingers with red
pepper (capsicum) rings or sprigs of rosemary,
if desired.

Barbecue the steaks on a rack over hot coals,
turning immediately the underside is sealed
(this is important to ensure juicy steaks).
Turn the steaks over frequently during
cooking until desired doneness is reached,
about 5 minutes on each side for rare. Serve
with small paper bun cases filled with
coleslaw. Garnish with sprigs of parsley, if
desired.

Serves 4.

LAMB CHOPS TAMARIND

BLUEBERRY VENISON

45 g (1½ oz/3 tablespoons) butter
1 onion, finely chopped
2 tablespoons tamarind concentrate
2 tablespoons tomato purée (paste)
2.5 cm (1 in) piece fresh ginger root, finely grated
2 teaspoons dark soft brown sugar
2 tablespoons olive oil
grated peel and juice of 1 large orange
6 double loin lamb chops
orange segments, orange peel and parsley sprigs, to garnish

Melt the butter in a saucepan and cook onion until transparent.

6 venison steaks
grated peel and juice of 2 oranges
juice of 1 lemon
3 tablespoons whisky
8 tablespoons olive oil
1 teaspoon rosemary leaves
3 bay leaves, crumbled
1 teaspoon celery salt
250 g (8 oz) blueberries
185 g (6 oz/1 cup) soft brown sugar
1 tablespoon lemon juice

Trim venison steaks and place on a chopping board. Flatten with a mallet or rolling pin.

Add tamarind concentrate, tomato purée (paste), ginger root, sugar, oil and orange peel and juice and simmer gently, uncovered, for 7-8 minutes until reduced by a quarter. Leave to cool. Coat the chops thoroughly in the sauce, then cover and refrigerate overnight.

Mix together orange peel and citrus juices, whisky, oil, rosemary, bay leaves and celery salt in a large, shallow dish. Place venison steaks in marinade, turning over to coat both sides. Leave in refrigerator for 6-8 hours, basting occasionally. Remove stalks from blueberries. In a heavy-based saucepan, combine sugar, remaining 1 tablespoon lemon juice and 155 ml (5 fl oz/⅔ cup) water. Heat gently, stirring until sugar dissolves. Add blueberries and bring to the boil. Reduce heat and cook until pulpy. Keep warm.

Grill the chops on a rack over hot coals for 15-20 minutes, turning twice during cooking and basting frequently with remaining sauce. If there is insufficient sauce for basting use a little olive oil instead. Serve garnished with orange segments and peel and parsley.

Serves 6.

Remove venison steaks from marinade and barbecue on an oiled rack over hot coals for about 10 seconds on each side to seal meat. Brush with marinade and continue cooking for 5-7 minutes on each side until tender. Serve with blueberry sauce.

Serves 6.

Note: Garnish each portion with a few bay leaves, blueberries and orange slices, if desired.

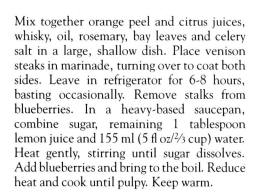

CHICKEN ST. LUCIA

60 g (2 oz/⅔ cup) creamed coconut, grated
1 teaspoon ground cumin
1 teaspoon ground cardamom
4 tablespoons mango chutney
125 ml (4 fl oz/½ cup) corn oil
1½-2 teaspoons salt
4 teaspoons turmeric
four 315-375 g (10-12 oz) chicken quarters

Heat 60 ml (2 fl oz/¼ cup) water in a small saucepan, stir in the grated coconut and when well blended, remove from the heat. Stir in the cumin, cardamom and mango chutney. Spoon the mixture into a bowl, cover and set aside.

Mix together the oil, salt and turmeric and brush generously all over the chicken quarters. Barbecue the chicken quarters on a rack over medium coals for 12-15 minutes on each side, basting frequently with the remaining seasoned oil. Pierce through to the bone with a skewer to make sure that the juices are clear and the chicken is fully cooked.

Serve with a tiny pot of the sauce on the side of the plate.

Serves 4.

CRANBERRY BALLOTINE

2 kg (4 lb) oven-ready chicken
1 onion, chopped
2 tablespoons oil
90 g (3 oz/½ cup) long-grain rice
220 ml (7 fl oz/⅞ cup) stock
90 g (3 oz/½ cup) raisins
grated peel and juice of 1 lemon
salt and pepper
1 egg, beaten
60 g (2 oz) cranberries, cooked and drained
½ teaspoon sugar

Remove chicken wings at second joint and reserve. Loosen skin at neck, cut around wishbone and remove.

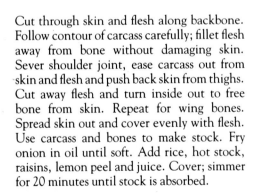

Cut through skin and flesh along backbone. Follow contour of carcass carefully; fillet flesh away from bone without damaging skin. Sever shoulder joint, ease carcass out from skin and flesh and push back skin from thighs. Cut away flesh and turn inside out to free bone from skin. Repeat for wing bones. Spread skin out and cover evenly with flesh. Use carcass and bones to make stock. Fry onion in oil until soft. Add rice, hot stock, raisins, lemon peel and juice. Cover; simmer for 20 minutes until stock is absorbed.

Season rice mixture to taste with salt and pepper. Cool, then beat in egg. Spread over flesh side of chicken, leaving a 2 cm (¾ in) border. Sweeten cranberries; spoon lengthwise along centre of rice. Re-shape and sew chicken. Roast on rack over low coals, in a covered barbecue, for 1-1¼ hours until chicken is dark golden brown. Leave to stand for 10-15 minutes before carving.

Serves 4.

CHICKEN TERIYAKI

750 g (1½ lb) boned, skinned chicken breasts
three 250 g (8 oz) cans water chestnuts
4 tablespoons dry sherry
4 tablespoons medium-dry white wine
4 tablespoons shoyu sauce
2 cloves garlic, crushed
sunflower oil for brushing
shredded lettuce, onion rings, parsley sprigs and
    paprika, to garnish, if desired

Cut the chicken into 2.5 cm (1 in) cubes. Drain water chestnuts and mix together in a dish.

In a small bowl, mix together sherry, wine, shoyu sauce and garlic. Pour over chicken and water chestnuts, cover and leave to marinate for 30-60 minutes, stirring occasionally. Using a slotted spoon, remove chicken cubes and water chestnuts from marinade. Thread pieces of chicken and water chestnuts alternately onto 8 long skewers. Reserve any remaining marinade.

Brush chicken and chestnuts with oil and barbecue on a rack over hot coals for about 10 minutes, turning frequently and basting with reserved marinade and oil. Arrange shredded lettuce on a large platter and place skewers in a criss-cross pattern on top. Garnish with raw onion rings, parsley and a sprinkling of paprika, if desired.

Serves 8.

CHICKEN LIVER KEBABS

625 g (1¼ lb) chicken livers, rinsed and trimmed
60 ml (2 fl oz/¼ cup) sunflower oil
1 onion, finely chopped
1 clove garlic, crushed
60 ml (2 fl oz/¼ cup) red wine
½ teaspoon Tabasco sauce
1½ teaspoons dark soft brown sugar
12 black peppercorns
salt
18 canned water chestnuts
1 large red pepper (capsicum), cored, seeded and sliced
    into rings

Halve or quarter chicken livers, depending on size.

Heat oil in a small saucepan and gently fry onion until soft. Add garlic, wine, Tabasco sauce, sugar and peppercorns and season with salt to taste. Bring to boil, add prepared livers and simmer for 1 minute to firm liver. Remove from heat and leave to marinate for 2 hours.

Using a slotted spoon, remove livers from marinade. Thread alternately onto 6 skewers, with the water chestnuts. Discard the peppercorns from marinade. Barbecue on rack over hot coals for 6-8 minutes, turning frequently and basting occasionally with marinade. Serve with red pepper (capsicum) rings, dressed with remaining marinade.

Serves 6.

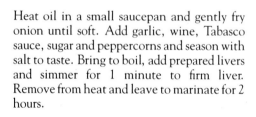

CHICKEN SATAY

2 tablespoons groundnut oil
1 large onion, finely chopped
3 cloves garlic, finely chopped
220 g (7 oz) creamed coconut
500 ml (16 fl oz/2 cups) hot water
2 tablespoons lemon juice
2 teaspoons salt
1 teaspoon ground cardamom
½ teaspoon ground ginger
2 teaspoons turmeric
125 g (4 oz/⅔ cup) unsalted peanuts, roasted,
  skinned and finely ground
750 g (1½ lb) raw chicken meat, cut into 2.5 cm (1 in)
  cubes
lemon slices or wedges and coriander sprigs, to garnish

Heat oil and gently fry onion and garlic until soft. In a large bowl, blend coconut with hot water and add lemon juice, salt, cardamom, ginger, turmeric and peanuts. Add cooked onion and garlic, including any oil left in pan. Add cubed chicken and stir well. Cover bowl, put in refrigerator and leave to marinate for 4 hours.

Remove cubed chicken from marinade and thread onto 8 skewers. Barbecue on rack over hot coals for 10-12 minutes, turning frequently and basting with remaining marinade. Serve garnished with lemon and coriander.

Serves 8.

Note: This dish is delicious served with prawn crackers which are obtainable from larger supermarkets, delicatessens, Chinese, Japanese and Asian food shops.

DEEP SOUTH DRUMSTICKS

12-16 chicken drumsticks
2.5 cm (1 in) slice wholemeal bread
6 tablespoons tomato purée (paste)
3 tablespoons full-bodied red wine
juice of ½ lemon
2 tablespoons Worcestershire sauce
2 tablespoons molasses
1 teaspoon salt
½ teaspoon pepper
1 teaspoon French mustard
½ teaspoon chilli powder
1 teaspoon paprika
2 tablespoons oil
parsley sprigs, to garnish

Wash and dry drumsticks and set aside.

Remove the crusts, then dice the bread. Put in a large shallow dish, with all the remaining ingredients, except parsley. Stir with a fork until the bread is incorporated. (The mixture with be thick.) Put the drumsticks into the sauce, twisting at the bone end to coat evenly. Leave in a cool place for 1 hour, turning drumsticks occasionally.

Wrap drumsticks individually in oiled, single thickness foil. Barbecue on a rack over medium hot coals for 30-40 minutes, turning the packets from time to time. Test 1 drumstick for doneness by pricking with a skewer – the juices should run clear and flesh touching the bone be fully cooked. Garnish with parsley and serve in the foil pockets with baby corn.

Serves 12-16.

SPATCHCOCKED CHICKEN

two 500 g (1 lb) oven-ready poussins or spring
  chickens
45 g (1½ oz/ 3 tablespoons) butter
¾ teaspoon grated lemon peel
¾ teaspoon dry mustard
90 ml (3 fl oz/⅓ cup) double (thick) cream
parsley sprigs, to garnish

On a wooden chopping board, and using
poultry shears or a heavy, sharp-bladed knife,
cut the birds through the backbone. With
skin-sides uppermost, flatten each bird to 2.5
cm (1 in) thickness using a mallet or rolling
pin.

Soften butter and blend in the lemon peel,
mustard and cream. Spread split chickens
with half the mixture. Diagonally insert 2
long skewers through both thighs and breast,
crossing them over in the centre.

Barbecue on a rack over hot coals for 20
minutes, basting occasionally with remaining
butter cream and turning once. Reduce heat
and move birds to side of barbecue. Continue
cooking for about 20 minutes, or until juices
run clear when pricked with a skewer, turning
once. Remove skewers and halve before
serving, garnished with parsley sprigs.

Serves 4.

POUSSIN AIOLI

5 cloves garlic, peeled
2 egg yolks
125 ml (4 fl oz/½ cup) olive oil
1 teaspoon lemon juice
salt and pepper
2 oven-ready poussins
lemon slices and parsley sprigs, to garnish

In a glass bowl, pound garlic to a pulp with a
pestle. Gradually beat in egg yolks.

Beat oil into mixture drop by drop until it
starts to thicken. Mix lemon juice with 1
teaspoon water and beat in alternate drops of
juice and oil until well incorporated. Season
to taste with salt and pepper.

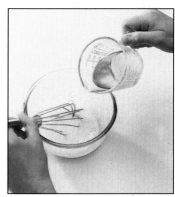

Loosen skin of poussins and, using a spoon
handle, spread garlic mayonnaise close to the
flesh. Brush mixture inside each cavity and
also over outside of birds. Separately wrap
each poussin in double thickness foil.
Barbecue on rack over medium coals for 30
minutes. Remove poussins from foil,
barbecue on rack for further 15-20 minutes,
turning and basting occasionally. Serve
poussins, whole or halved, garnished with
lemon and parsley.

Serves 2-4.

SAUCY SPIT-ROAST DUCKLING

2 kg (4½ lb) oven-ready duckling
salt and pepper
155 ml (5 fl oz/⅔ cup) pineapple juice

SAUCE: 500 g (1 lb) stoned black cherries
1 clove garlic, unskinned
155 ml (5 fl oz/⅔ cup) port
470 ml (15 fl oz/1¾ cups) well-flavoured, strong beef
 stock
1 tablespoon fecule or potato flour
30 g (1 oz/6 teaspoons) butter
1 tablespoon redcurrant jelly

Prick duck skin in several places. Season inside and out with salt and pepper. Sprinkle inside with a little pineapple juice.

To make sauce, put cherries, garlic, port and stock in a saucepan and poach until cherries are tender. Remove cherries with a slotted spoon and set aside. Discard garlic. Blend fecule or potato flour with 2 tablespoons cold water, stir into liquid in pan and bring to boil, stirring continuously until thickened. Mix in butter, redcurrant jelly and salt and pepper to taste. Add cherries and cook until hot. Reheat on side of barbecue when duck is cooked.

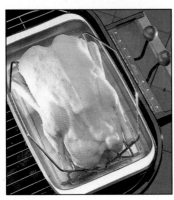

When the barbecue coals are hot move them towards side and place a roasting tin in centre. This must be large enough to catch drips (which are considerable). Fix duck onto a spit or put in a roasting basket. Barbecue over medium heat for 2½-3 hours until well cooked. Foil tenting or covering with barbecue lid will hasten cooking. Do not open for 30 minutes, then baste every 10 minutes with pineapple juice. Pour away fat; mix juices into sauce and serve with duck.

Serves 6-8.

CHINESE DUCK

three 500 g (1 lb) duck breast quarters
hoisin sauce
bunch spring onions, trimmed and shredded lengthwise

MARINADE: 2 teaspoons miso paste
90 ml (3 fl oz/⅓ cup) dry sherry or saki
¼-½ teaspoon five-spice-powder

CHINESE PANCAKES: 250 g (8 oz/2 cups) strong white
 flour
185 ml (6 fl oz/¾ cup) boiling water
sesame oil

Deeply score the duck flesh through to the bone in a criss-cross fashion. Thoroughly blend the marinade ingredients together.

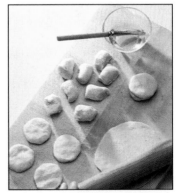

Put duck in a dish; add marinade. Cover; chill for 12 hours, basting occasionally. Make pancakes. Put flour in bowl; add boiling water and mix to a dough. Knead for 10 minutes. Cover with damp cloth and leave for 30 minutes. Knead for 5 minutes; divide into 16 pieces. Work with 2 pieces at a time; press out to 5 cm (2 in) diameter. Oil one side of each piece; sandwich oiled sides together. With a rolling pin, press out to 17.5 cm (7 in) circles. Cook in an ungreased pan over low heat for 1-1½ minutes per side until opaque and pale yellow. Peel apart.

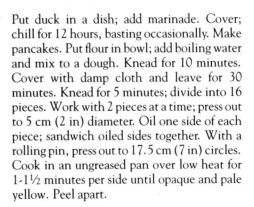

Barbecue the duck quarters on a rack over low coals in a covered barbecue for about 1 hour, turning them over 3 times during cooking and basting with any remaining marinade. If using an unlidded barbecue, tent with foil and allow extra time. Shred the meat from the bone while duck is still hot. Serve a portion of shredded duck with 3 or 4 pancakes, a tiny dish of hoisin sauce and the onions. The pancakes are eaten spread with sauce and filled with duck and onions.

Serves 3-4.

GINGER & APRICOT CHICKEN

PIQUANT SPRING CHICKEN

8-10 unboned, unskinned fresh chicken thighs
411 g (14½ oz) can apricot halves in natural juice
about 250 ml (8 fl oz/ 1 cup) natural orange juice
1 tablespoon walnut oil
1 small slice onion, minced
1 teaspoon grated fresh ginger root
salt and pepper
16 red cherries, stoned

Deeply slash the chicken thighs to the bone
in 2 or 3 places.

two 560 g (1 lb 2 oz) spring chickens
375 ml (12 fl oz/1½ cups) tomato juice
60 ml (2 fl oz/¼ cup) Worcestershire sauce
2 teaspoons lemon juice
juice of ½ orange
salt and pepper
4 heads chicory
knob of butter
1 orange, thinly sliced, to garnish

Halve the chickens so that each has a wing
and a leg. Place cut-side up in a shallow dish.

Remove the apricot halves from the juice,
reserve 16 for garnish and mash the
remainder. Make the juice up to 375 ml (12
fl oz/1½ cups) with orange juice. Pour into a
large bowl, add the oil, mashed apricots,
onion and ginger and season to taste with salt
and pepper. Mix in the chicken thighs, cover
and leave in a cool place for 2 hours, stirring
occasionally.

Combine the tomato juice, Worcestershire
sauce and citrus juices. Season generously
with pepper. Pour over the chicken, cover
and refrigerate for 12 hours, basting
occasionally. Put the chicory heads on
individual pieces of double thickness foil. Dot
with butter and season to taste with salt and
pepper. Wrap tightly.

Barbecue the chicken thighs on an oiled rack
over hot coals for 25-30 minutes, turning
them over 2 or 3 times and basting with the
remaining marinade. Place the reserved
apricot halves on a foil tray on the barbecue
for 3-5 minutes to warm. Fill with the
cherries and serve with the chicken thighs.

Serves 4.

Barbecue the chickens on an oiled rack over
medium coals for 30-40 minutes until well
cooked, basting occasionally with the
marinade. Cook chicory parcels over or in
medium coals during the final 10-12 minutes.
Garnish the chicken halves with orange
slices and serve with the chicory parcels.

Serves 4.

CAPERED NEW POTATOES

500 g (1 lb) new potatoes
3 tablespoons capers
90 g (3 oz/⅓ cup) butter, softened
parsley sprigs, to garnish

Scrub potatoes well, then boil in their skins in salted water for 10 minutes. Drain and leave to cool slightly

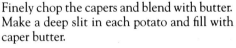

Finely chop the capers and blend with butter. Make a deep slit in each potato and fill with caper butter.

Tightly wrap each potato in separate squares of single thickness foil and barbecue on rack over hot coals for 10-15 minutes. Garnish with sprigs of parsley.

Serves 4-6.

Note: These barbecued potatoes are ideal as an accompaniment to plain grilled fish or poultry.

WHOLE TOMATOES IN WINE

8 firm tomatoes
8 teaspoons red wine
salt and pepper
watercress or lettuce leaves, to serve, if desired

Cut 8 large squares of double thickness foil. Cup each tomato in foil but do not completely enclose.

Pour over 1 teaspoon wine and season to taste with salt and pepper. Mould foil around tomatoes securely to prevent juices escaping.

Put packets on side of rack over medium coals and cook for about 10-15 minutes. Unwrap and transfer to serving plates, spooning wine-flavoured juices over tomatoes. Serve on a bed of watercress or lettuce leaves, if desired.

Serves 8.

Note: The tomatoes are particularly delicious as an accompaniment to barbecued steaks or burgers which can be cooked at the same time.

HOT HOT ALOO

500 g (1 lb) small new potatoes
12 teaspoons lime pickle
60 ml (2 fl oz/¼ cup) salad oil
2 teaspoons tomato purée (paste)
2 teaspoons ground cardamom
2 tablespoons natural yogurt
lime slices, to garnish

Wash and scrub potatoes. Cook in salted water until tender but firm. Drain. Leave until cold, then thread onto 4-6 skewers.

Put lime pickle in a glass bowl and using kitchen scissors, cut up any large pieces of the pickle. Blend in oil, tomato purée (paste), cardamom and yogurt.

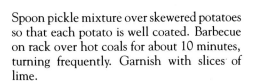

Spoon pickle mixture over skewered potatoes so that each potato is well coated. Barbecue on rack over hot coals for about 10 minutes, turning frequently. Garnish with slices of lime.

Serves 4-6.

Note: Use mild lime pickle, if preferred.

SWEET & SOUR AUBERGINES

2 aubergines (eggplants)
3 tablespoons tarragon vinegar
3 tablespoons olive oil
1 small clove garlic, crushed
pinch of salt
½ teaspoon French mustard
1 tablespoon chopped fresh parsley
½ teaspoon dried marjoram
pinch of cayenne pepper
1 tablespoon sugar
marjoram sprigs, to garnish

Peel aubergines (eggplants), cut in half, then slice and cut into 2.5 cm (1 in) cubes.

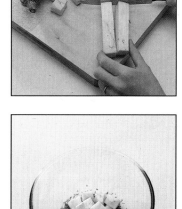

Combine remaining ingredients, except garnish, in a large bowl, add cubed aubergine (eggplant) and mix well. Leave for 15 minutes, stirring occasionally.

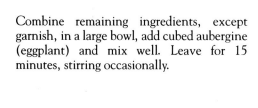

Thread onto 8 skewers and barbecue over hot coals for 15 minutes, turning occasionally. Garnish with sprigs of marjoram.

Serves 8.

Note: These are extremely good served with grilled steaks or chops.

COUNTY MUSHROOMS

SPANISH CHARCOALED ONIONS

12 open, flat mushrooms, each weighing about
   60 g (2 oz)
185 ml (6 fl oz/¾ cup) virgin olive oil
60 ml (2 fl oz/¼ cup) lemon juice
5 teaspoons grated horseradish
¼ teaspoon salt
¼ teaspoon pepper
1 tablespoon chopped fresh parsley, to garnish

Wipe mushrooms and, if needed, cut stalks to
1 cm (½ in) lengths.

2 large Spanish or red onions
garlic salt
4 tablespoons double (thick) cream, half-whipped
1 tablespoon crushed black peppercorns
30 g (1 oz/6 teaspoons) butter
rosemary sprigs, to garnish

Peel onions and cut into 1 cm (½ in) thick
slices. Do not separate into rings.

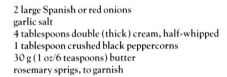

Thoroughly mix olive oil, lemon juice, grated
horseradish and salt and pepper in a large
shallow dish. Add mushrooms, spooning
liquid over to completely coat. Leave to stand
for at least 30 minutes, basting occasionally.

Season to taste with garlic salt. Brush one
side with double (thick) cream and sprinkle
with crushed peppercorns.

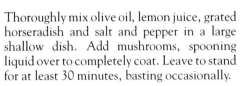

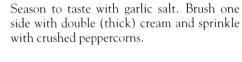

Barbecue on rack over hot coals for about 10
minutes, turning over and basting
occasionally. Garnish open sides of
mushrooms with chopped parsley.

Serves 6-12.

Barbecue in a tented, hinged wire basket and
cook cream-side up first. Barbecue over hot
coals for 5-8 minutes on each side until
beginning to 'charcoal'. Put dabs of butter on
surface of onion slices while first sides are
cooking. Serve peppered-sides up, garnished
with sprigs of rosemary.

Makes 8-10.

Note: Serve with meat dishes, or as an
appetiser.

SINGED SPICED PLANTAINS

6 plantains or under-ripe bananas
30 g (1 oz/6 teaspoons) butter
2 tablespoons lemon juice
½ teaspoon quatre épices
pinch of ground ginger
lemon slices, to garnish

Without peeling, barbecue the plantains or bananas over medium coals, turning them over until the skin blackens.

Soften the butter, mix in the lemon juice, quatre épices and ginger.

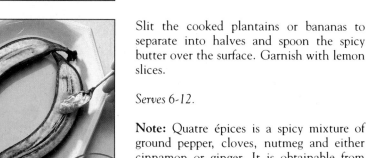

Slit the cooked plantains or bananas to separate into halves and spoon the spicy butter over the surface. Garnish with lemon slices.

Serves 6-12.

Note: Quatre épices is a spicy mixture of ground pepper, cloves, nutmeg and either cinnamon or ginger. It is obtainable from many delicatessens.

Singed Spiced Plantains are delicious served with chicken, gammon or veal dishes.

SAGE & CREAM JACKETS

6 baking potatoes
vegetable oil
2 tablespoons white wine vinegar
1 bunch spring onions, finely sliced
1 egg yolk
pinch of dry mustard
salt and pepper
1 teaspoon sage leaves, finely chopped
155 ml (5 fl oz/⅔ cup) thick sour cream
fresh sage leaves, to garnish

Scrub potatoes and dry on absorbent kitchen paper. Prick deeply through skins and rub with oil.

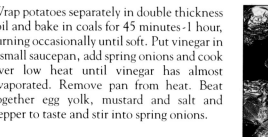

Wrap potatoes separately in double thickness foil and bake in coals for 45 minutes-1 hour, turning occasionally until soft. Put vinegar in a small saucepan, add spring onions and cook over low heat until vinegar has almost evaporated. Remove pan from heat. Beat together egg yolk, mustard and salt and pepper to taste and stir into spring onions.

Cook over very low heat for 1 minute, beating continuously until mixture thickens. Care must be taken not to overheat or sauce may curdle. Remove from heat; stir in chopped sage and cream. Cut a deep cross through foil into cooked potatoes and squeeze sides to open out. Spoon in a little sauce. Garnish with sage leaves.

Serves 6.

COURGETTES WITH HERBS

8-10 young firm courgettes (zucchini), about 12 cm (5 in) long
1 teaspoon lemon verbena leaves
4-5 fresh mint leaves
1 teaspoon marjoram leaves
2 bay leaves
½ teaspoon salt
2 tablespoons medium white wine
2 tablespoons lemon juice
4 tablespoons sunflower oil
lemon slices and fresh herbs, to garnish

Rinse and dry courgettes (zucchini) and pierce at either end and in one or two places along length. Finely chop herbs.

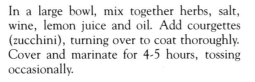

In a large bowl, mix together herbs, salt, wine, lemon juice and oil. Add courgettes (zucchini), turning over to coat thoroughly. Cover and marinate for 4-5 hours, tossing occasionally.

Remove courgettes (zucchini) from marinade and barbecue on rack over hot coals for about 8-10 minutes until tender, but not soft, turning frequently and basting with remaining marinade. Serve skewered with wooden sticks. Garnish with lemon slices and fresh herbs.

Serves 8-10.

WALNUT APPLE CRESCENTS

2 small, red-skinned eating apples
30 g (1 oz/⅓ cup) shelled walnuts
30 g (1 oz) block dried dates
60 ml (2 fl oz/¼ cup) apple juice
1 teaspoon grated orange peel
strips of orange peel, to garnish

Rinse and dry apples and remove core, keeping apples whole. Cut each apple in half lengthwise. (Each half will have a tubular shaped hollow along centre.)

Roughly chop walnuts and dates. Put apple juice and grated orange peel in a small saucepan. Add walnuts and dates, bring to boil, then simmer for 2-3 minutes until liquid has been absorbed. Cool slightly, then fill apple hollows with mixture.

Wrap each apple half separately in double thickness foil. Barbecue on rack over hot coals for about 30 minutes, turning occasionally until apples are tender. Garnish with strips of orange peel.

Serves 4.

Note: Serve as an accompaniment to poultry or game.

SKEWERED POTATO CRISPS

two 250 g (8 oz) baking potatoes
hot water
salt
4 tablespoons sunflower oil

Peel potatoes. Carefully cut into paper thin slices lengthwise, following the curve of the potato.

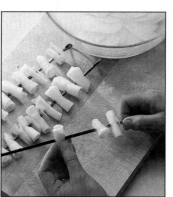

Immediately plunge potato slices into hot, salted water. Stir to separate, then leave for 3-4 minutes until pliable. Carefully coil each potato slice, then thread onto long skewers, leaving at least 1 cm (½ in) space between each one.

Brush potato coils with oil and grill on rack over hot coals for 10-15 minutes, turning frequently until potato coils are crisp. Briefly lay skewers on kitchen paper to drain before serving.

Serves 4-6.

Note: The recipe may be doubled, but it will then be better to soak potato slices in separate bowls of hot, salted water.

PEANUT BEEF TOMATOES

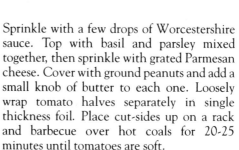

4 beef tomatoes
salt and pepper
few drops Worcestershire sauce
2 teaspoons chopped fresh basil
2 teaspoons chopped fresh parsley
4 teaspoons grated Parmesan cheese
60 g (2 oz) roasted unsalted peanuts, finely ground
knob of butter
8 bracelets of fried bread (see Note)
basil or parsley sprigs, to garnish

Rinse and dry tomatoes and halve crosswise. Season the cut surfaces of tomatoes with salt and pepper.

Sprinkle with a few drops of Worcestershire sauce. Top with basil and parsley mixed together, then sprinkle with grated Parmesan cheese. Cover with ground peanuts and add a small knob of butter to each one. Loosely wrap tomato halves separately in single thickness foil. Place cut-sides up on a rack and barbecue over hot coals for 20-25 minutes until tomatoes are soft.

Remove from foil wrappings and place each tomato in centre of a fried croûton bracelet. Garnish with basil or parsley sprigs.

Serves 4-8.

Note: The bracelets can be prepared ahead of time and will store in the freezer. Re-crisp on barbecue at the last minute. To make the bracelets, cut out 8 rounds of bread from a sliced loaf and use a slightly smaller cutter to remove centres. Fry in shallow oil. Drain thoroughly.

CRUSTY GARLIC POTATOES

ROAST CORN ON THE COB

500 g (1 lb) new potatoes
8-10 large cloves garlic
2 eggs, beaten
6-8 tablespoons yellow cornmeal
parsley sprigs, to garnish

6 corn cobs, with husks
125 g (4 oz/½ cup) butter, melted

HERBED BUTTER PATS: 60 g (2 oz/¼ cup) butter
1 teaspoon lemon juice
2 tablespoons chopped fresh parsley
1 tablespoon chopped fresh chives
salt and pepper

Scrub potatoes well. Peel garlic, leaving the cloves whole.

Fold back corn husks, pull out silk from corn and re-wrap husks over corn. Soak in cold water for at least 1 hour. Drain cobs and shake off surplus water.

Boil potatoes and garlic in salted water for 12-15 minutes until just cooked. Drain, reserving garlic. Skin potatoes as soon as they are cool enough to handle. Roughly chop garlic and, using a small skewer, insert pieces deeply into potatoes.

While cobs are soaking, prepare the butter pats. Beat all ingredients together until softened and well blended. Shape into a 2.5 cm (1 in) wide roll and wrap tightly in grease-proof paper, maintaining cylindrical shape. Chill in freezer until firm, then slice. Arrange in a single layer on a plate and refrigerate until needed.

Dip potatoes first in beaten egg and then in cornmeal. Press on well with a round-bladed knife, then dip in beaten egg once more. Barbecue on a well-oiled rack over hot coals for 10-15 minutes until crusty and golden. Serve in a basket lined with a clean napkin. Garnish with sprigs of parsley.

Serves 5-6.

Pull back corn husks and brush corn with melted butter. Re-wrap corn in husks and barbecue on a rack over medium coals for 30-40 minutes, turning frequently until the husks are well browned. Remove husks and serve corn with the butter pats.

Serves 6.

Variation: After brushing corn cobs with melted butter in step 3, corn cobs may also be spread with peanut butter, if desired.

CHIVE & GARLIC BREAD

1 French loaf
3 cloves garlic
¼ teaspoon salt
125 g (4 oz/½ cup) butter
2 tablespoons chopped fresh chives

Slice loaf diagonally and deeply at about 2 cm (¾ in) intervals, but do not cut through completely.

Peel garlic, place on a piece of greaseproof paper, sprinkle with salt and crush with flat side of a table knife. Soften butter, blend in garlic and mix in chives. Spread garlic butter between slices, covering both sides generously.

Re-shape loaf and wrap securely in foil. Place on rack and barbecue over hot coals for 10-15 minutes, turning parcel over several times. Open foil and serve at once.

Serves 6.

BROCCOLI PANCAKE ROLLS

250 g (8 oz) broccoli spears
90 ml (3 fl oz/⅓ cup) natural Greek yogurt
pepper
2 tablespoons plain flour
3 tablespoons milk
4 large eggs
1 tablespoon soy sauce
butter
vegetable oil

Cook broccoli in a little boiling, salted water for 6-8 minutes. Drain well and chop finely. Mix with yogurt and season well with black pepper. Cover and set aside.

Sift flour into a mixing bowl and blend in milk. Beat eggs and soy sauce together and add gradually to flour mixture, beating well to form a smooth, thin batter. Pour into a jug. Heat a small omelette pan, add a knob of butter and make six or eight 15 cm (6 in) thin omelette-style pancakes, browning them on one side only. (If necessary, grease pan with a little butter after making each pancake.) Remove pancakes carefully (they set as they cool) and spread out, cooked-sides up, on non-stick paper.

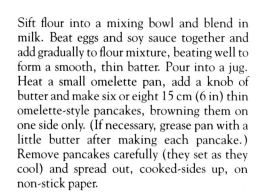

Spoon a little of the broccoli filling on one edge of the browned side of each pancake. Fold over to enclose filling, tucking in sides and fold again to form a parcel. Brush cool pancake rolls with oil and bake, starting with seam-sides down, over hot coals for 3-4 minutes on each side.

Serves 6-8.

Note: These pancake rolls taste delicious served with a green salad.

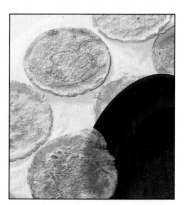

SALADS

DUCK WITH KUMQUATS

90 g (3 oz) young spinach leaves, trimmed
4 duck breast fillets, skinned
155 ml (5 fl oz/⅔ cup) dry white wine
pinch ground ginger
8 coriander seeds, crushed
salt and pepper
12 kumquats, sliced
3 tablespoons hazelnut oil
2 teaspoons lemon juice
pomegranate seeds, to garnish

Wash and dry spinach and arrange on 4 plates.

Put duck breasts into a frying pan and pour over the wine. Add ginger and coriander. Season with salt and pepper. Cover pan and simmer for 10 minutes until duck is tender. Add kumquats and simmer for 1 minute. Remove duck and kumquats from pan with a slotted spoon and set aside.

Simmer the liquid in the pan until reduced to 60 ml (2 fl oz/¼ cup). Stir in oil and lemon juice and warm through.

Slice the duck and arrange on the plates with the kumquats. Pour over dressing, then serve garnished with pomegranate seeds.

Serves 4 as a main course.

PEPPERY CHICKEN SALAD

60 g (2 oz) lollo rosso or radicchio
¼ head curly endive
60 g (2 oz) lamb's lettuce
4 tomatoes, skinned
4 chicken breasts (fillets), skinned
315 ml (10 fl oz/1¼ cups) dry white wine
salt and pepper
1½ teaspoons green peppercorns in brine, drained
75 ml (2½ fl oz/⅓ cup) single (light) cream

Wash and dry salad leaves, tear any large ones into smaller pieces, then divide between 4 plates. Cut each tomato into 8 wedges, remove seeds, then arrange over the lettuce leaves on the plates.

Put chicken breasts into a frying pan, pour over wine and season with salt and pepper. Poach for 15 minutes until chicken is tender. Lift out of pan with slotted spoon, place on a chopping board and slice.

Add the peppercorns to the cooking liquid, then boil rapidly until liquid is reduced to 5 tablespoons. Stir in cream and warm through. Arrange the chicken on the salad, pour over cream dressing and serve immediately.

Serves 4 as a main course.

HOT SAUSAGE SALAD

185 g (6 oz) finely shredded red cabbage
185 g (6 oz) finely shredded white cabbage
1 cooking apple
1 teaspoon lemon juice
1 pork boiling ring sausage
1 tablespoon chopped fresh parsley, to garnish
MUSTARD MAYONNAISE:
2 tablespoons Mayonnaise
2 tablespoons low fat soft cheese
2 teaspoons wholegrain mustard
2 teaspoons apple juice
salt and pepper

Put shredded cabbage into a bowl and mix together. Grate apple, toss with lemon juice, then add to cabbage.

Cook sausage according to packet directions. Meanwhile, make mayonnaise by mixing ingredients together in a bowl. Stir into cabbage, then spoon onto 4 plates.

Slice cooked sausage and arrange over salad. Garnish with parsley.

Serves 4 as a main course.

THAI SEAFOOD SALAD

250 g (8 oz) monkfish, skinned and cubed
4 scallops, thawed if frozen
250 g (8 oz) salmon steak, skinned and cubed
8 raw Mediterranean (king) prawns
5 cm (2 in) piece fresh ginger, shredded
2 bulbs lemon grass, peeled and chopped
spring onion curls, to garnish
MARINADE:
juice of 1 lime
4 teaspoons light soy sauce
2 teaspoons chopped fresh mint
3 teaspoons chopped fresh coriander
1 clove garlic, crushed
WILD RICE SALAD:
45 g (1½ oz/3 tablespoons) wild rice
2.5 cm (1 in) piece fresh ginger, halved
45 g (1½ oz/3 tablespoons) long grain rice
1 tablespoon light sesame oil
6 coriander seeds, crushed

Put all seafood onto a plate, scatter ginger and lemon grass over the top.

Place an upturned saucer in a wok, add 1 cupful of water. Stand plate on saucer. Cover and steam for 5-6 minutes until the seafood is cooked. Or, use a steamer.

To make marinade, mix ingredients together in large bowl. Add cooked fish with 2 tablespoons of cooking juices. Stir gently, then leave to marinate for at least 1 hour.

To make rice salad, put wild rice and ginger into a saucepan of simmering water and cook for 30 minutes. Add long grain rice, cook a further 20 minutes until tender.

Drain rice and discard the ginger. Stir in sesame oil and coriander seeds. Divide rice between 4 plates, arrange fish on top and spoon over marinade. Garnish with spring onion curls.

Serves 4.

SALAD NIÇOISE

125 g (4 oz) thin green beans, trimmed
6 tomatoes, quartered
½ cucumber, peeled and diced
1 red pepper (capsicum), seeded and sliced
6 spring onions, chopped
220 g (7 oz) can tuna fish, drained and flaked
90 g (3 oz) black olives, stoned
1 tablespoon chopped fresh parsley
3 eggs, hard-boiled
60 g (2 oz) can anchovies, drained
MUSTARD VINAIGRETTE DRESSING:
60 ml (2 fl oz/¼ cup) extra virgin olive oil
1 tablespoon red wine vinegar
1 tablespoon lemon juice
¼ teaspoon Dijon mustard
salt and pepper

Cook beans in a saucepan of water for 5-6 minutes, until just tender. Drain, rinse under cold water, then cut into 4 cm (1½ in) lengths. Put into a bowl with tomatoes, cucumber, red pepper (capsicum), spring onions, tuna fish and olives. Mix together.

To make dressing, mix ingredients together in a bowl or screw-top jar, add to the salad with the parsley and toss gently. Quarter the hard-boiled eggs and arrange on the salad. Cut anchovy fillets in half lengthwise and arrange in criss-cross patterns on top of salad.

Serves 4.

MALAYSIAN SALAD

250 g (8 oz) white cabbage, shredded
125 g (4 oz) thin green beans, cut into 2.5 cm (1 in) lengths
½ small cauliflower, divided into flowerets
125 g (4 oz) beansprouts, trimmed
½ cucumber
coriander leaves, to garnish
PEANUT SAUCE:
30 g (1 oz) desiccated coconut
155 ml (5 fl oz/⅔ cup) boiling water
3 tablespoons peanut butter
2 teaspoons soy sauce
juice of ½ lime
¼ teaspoon chilli powder

To make sauce, place coconut in a bowl, pour over boiling water and leave to soak for 15 minutes.

Bring a large saucepan of water to the boil, add cabbage, beans and cauliflower and simmer for 2-3 minutes. Drain vegetables thoroughly, arrange on a platter or 4 individual plates. Scatter over beansprouts. Cut strips of skin from cucumber with a canelle knife, then slice the cucumber and arrange over salad.

Strain coconut milk into a bowl, discard the coconut, and add remaining sauce ingredients; mix well. Spoon onto centre of salad or serve separately. Garnish the salad with coriander leaves.

Serves 4.

PASTA PESTO SALAD

250 g (8 oz) orzo (rice-shaped pasta)

250 g (8 oz) cherry tomatoes, quartered

30 g (1 oz) pine nuts, lightly toasted

basil sprigs, to garnish

PESTO DRESSING:

30 g (1 oz) fresh basil leaves

2 cloves garlic, peeled

30 g (1 oz) pine nuts

3 tablespoons virgin olive oil

30 g (1 oz/¼ cup) grated Parmesan cheese

3 tablespoons single (light) cream

Cook pasta in boiling salted water until just tender. Drain, rinse under cold water and drain again. Put into a bowl with the tomatoes.

To make the dressing, wash and dry basil leaves, then put into a blender or food processor with garlic, pine nuts and oil and work until smooth. Turn into a bowl, and beat in Parmesan cheese and cream. Stir into the pasta, then transfer to a serving dish. Serve the salad sprinkled with toasted pine nuts and garnished with a few sprigs of basil.

Serves 4.

ITALIAN SALAMI SALAD

470 g (15 oz) can haricot or cannellini beans, drained

1 bulb fennel, finely sliced

1 small green pepper (capsicum), seeded and diced

125 g (4 oz) Italian salami, sliced

basil leaves, tomato wedges and black olives, to garnish

GARLIC DRESSING:

3 tablespoons extra virgin olive oil

1 tablespoon white wine vinegar

1 clove garlic, crushed with salt

pepper

Put beans, fennel and green pepper (capsicum) into a bowl. Cut salami slices into quarters and add to the salad.

To make the dressing, mix ingredients together in a bowl or screw-top jar. Pour over the salad and toss together gently.

Spoon onto a serving dish and serve garnished with basil, tomato wedges and olives.

Serves 4.

STROGANOFF SALAD

375 g (12 oz) cold, rare cooked beef

250 g (8 oz) button mushrooms, sliced

6 spring onions, chopped or shredded

1 red pepper (capsicum), seeded and sliced

shredded lettuce, to serve

SOUR CREAM DRESSING:

155 ml (5 fl oz/⅔ cup) thick sour cream

1 tablespoon horseradish sauce

2 teaspoons lemon juice

salt and pepper

Cut the beef into thin strips and put into a bowl with the mushrooms, onions and pepper (capsicum).

To make the dressing, mix ingredients together in a bowl. Pour over the salad and toss gently. Line a serving dish with shredded lettuce and spoon salad on top.

Serves 4.

SPANISH PAELLA SALAD

2 tablespoons olive oil

1 onion, chopped

1 clove garlic, crushed

375 g (12 oz/ 2 cups) arborio (risotto) rice

pinch saffron threads

750 ml (24 fl oz/3 cups) hot chicken stock

250 g (8 oz) tomatoes, skinned, seeded and chopped

125 g (4 oz) cooked frozen peas

2 cooked skinned chicken breasts (fillets), diced

185 g (6 oz) chorizo sausage, skinned and sliced

1 red or green pepper (capsicum), seeded and sliced

stuffed olives, to garnish

PAPRIKA LEMON DRESSING:

3 tablespoons extra virgin olive oil

1 tablespoon lemon juice

½ teaspoon paprika

salt and pepper

Put oil in a large saucepan, add onion and garlic and cook gently for 5 minutes until soft. Stir in rice and cook for 2 minutes.

Stir in the saffron threads and hot stock and simmer until rice is tender and all liquid has been absorbed. Remove from the heat, transfer to a bowl and allow to cool completely.

To make the dressing, mix all the ingredients together in a bowl or screw-top jar.

Add the skinned chopped tomatoes, peas, chicken, sausage and pepper (capsicum) to rice. Pour the dressing over the salad, stir gently and serve garnished with stuffed olives.

Serves 4.

EGGS TONNATO

6 large eggs, hard-boiled	
1 canned pimento, cut into strips	
60 g (2 oz) anchovies, drained	
dill sprigs, to garnish	
TONNATO SAUCE:	
1 quantity Mayonnaise	
100 g (3½ oz) can tuna fish, drained	
1 tablespoon lemon juice	
1 tablespoon single (light) cream or	
natural yogurt	
1 teaspoon capers, drained and chopped	

To make sauce, put mayonnaise into a blender or food processor with tuna fish, lemon juice and single (light) cream or natural yogurt and work until smooth. Stir in the capers.

Halve eggs lengthwise and arrange on 4 plates. Spoon the sauce over the eggs and decorate with strips of pimento. Halve the anchovy fillets, then curl them round and place between the eggs. Serve the eggs garnished with sprigs of dill.

Serves 4.

PASTA & PRAWN SALAD

250 g (8 oz) pasta shells	
375 g (12 oz) peeled cooked prawns	
125 g (4 oz) smoked salmon, cut into strips	
tarragon sprigs, to garnish	
HERB DRESSING:	
3 tablespoons virgin olive oil	
1 tablespoon lemon juice	
1 tablespoon tomato juice	
1 tablespoon chopped fresh parsley	
1 tablespoon chopped fresh tarragon	
salt and pepper	

Cook pasta in boiling salted water until just tender. Drain, rinse under cold water and drain again. Put into a bowl with prawns and salmon.

To make the dressing, mix ingredients together in a bowl or screw-top jar. Pour over the salad, toss gently, then transfer to a serving dish. Serve garnished with sprigs of tarragon.

Serves 4.

BARBECUED STEAK SALAD

four 185 g (6 oz) fillet steaks
mixed salad leaves
cherry tomatoes, to garnish
MARINADE:
60 ml (2 fl oz/¼ cup) sunflower oil
2 tablespoons red wine vinegar
1 tablespoon tomato purée (paste)
2 teaspoons Worcestershire sauce
1 teaspoon Dijon mustard
1 clove garlic, crushed
½ teaspoon paprika
salt and pepper
AVOCADO DRESSING:
1 ripe avocado
juice of 1 lemon
60 ml (2 fl oz/¼ cup) virgin olive oil
1 clove garlic, crushed
60 ml (2 fl oz/¼ cup) single (light) cream

To make the marinade, put all the ingredients into a dish and mix together. Add the steaks, turn to coat then leave for 1 hour.

To make the dressing, halve the avocado, remove stone and scoop out flesh. Place in blender or food processor with remaining ingredients and work until smooth. Season with salt and pepper.

Arrange salad leaves on 4 plates. Either cook steaks on a barbecue or under a hot grill for 6-8 minutes, turning them once. Transfer cooked steaks to a board, slice them into strips and arrange on the plates. Spoon over dressing. Serve garnished with cherry tomatoes.

Serves 4.

Note: The dressing should be used within 2 hours of being made.

HERRINGSALAT

4 fresh herrings, cleaned, scaled and backbone removed
2 pickled gherkins, diced
250 g (8 oz) cooked potatoes, diced
½ bunch spring onions, chopped
250 g (8 oz) cooked beetroot, sliced
chives, to garnish
CIDER MARINADE:
125 ml (4 fl oz/½ cup) cider vinegar
125 ml (4 fl oz/½ cup) water
2 tablespoons sugar
1 small onion, chopped
1 bay leaf
good pinch pepper
good pinch allspice
YOGURT MAYONNAISE DRESSING:
6 tablespoons natural yogurt
2 tablespoons Mayonnaise

Cut herring fillets into 5 cm (2 in) pieces and put into a glass dish.

To prepare the marinade, combine ingredients in a saucepan and bring to the boil. Simmer for 1 minute, then leave to cool. Pour over herrings, and marinate overnight or for at least 6 hours.

Drain herrings from marinade and put into a bowl with gherkins, potatoes and spring onions. To make the dressing, mix ingredients together, then stir into salad.

Arrange sliced beetroot around edge of serving dish, spoon salad in centre and garnish with chives.

Serves 4.

SMOKED MACKEREL SALAD

500 g (1 lb) new potatoes
1 tablespoon olive oil
4 smoked mackerel fillets
½ cucumber, peeled
parsley sprigs, to garnish
MUSTARD DRESSING:
2 tablespoons sunflower oil
1 tablespoon wholegrain mustard
1 tablespoon lemon juice

In a saucepan of boiling water, cook potatoes in their skins until tender; drain. When cool enough to handle, remove skins, slice potatoes thickly, or quarter. Put into a bowl and toss with olive oil.

Remove skin from mackerel and discard. Break fish into pieces and add to potatoes. Cut cucumber in half crosswise; dice one half and add to salad.

To make the dressing, mix ingredients together in a bowl or screw-top jar. Stir into the salad, then spoon onto a serving dish. Using an apple corer, remove centre from remaining piece of cucumber and discard. Slice cucumber. Serve the salad garnished with cucumber slices and parsley.

Serves 4.

DRESSED CRAB

500 g (1 lb) cooked crab
1 teaspoon lemon juice
1 tablespoon Mayonnaise
30 g (1 oz/½ cup) fresh breadcrumbs
salt and pepper
1 egg, hard-boiled
1 tablespoon chopped fresh parsley
lettuce leaves and lemon slices, to garnish
extra mayonnaise, to serve

Hold crab firmly, twist off two claws and legs. Pull body section from shell, discarding feathery gills, the greyish-white stomach sac behind the head and any green matter.

Using a teaspoon, scrape into a bowl all brown meat inside shell. Discard inner membrane attached on either side. Press natural dark line on underside of shell to break along the line neatly; discard the broken inner shell. Wash and dry the main shell.

Snap legs in half by bending backwards at joint. Using a hammer, gently crack all shells; scrape white meat into a second bowl, using a skewer to get into crevices. Discard any bits of shell. Crack large claws, remove meat and add to bowl.

Cut body section in half, pick out white meat from honeycomb structure and add to bowl.

To dress the crab, mix brown meat with lemon juice, mayonnaise and breadcrumbs and season with salt and pepper. Flake white meat with fork. Spoon brown mixture in a line in centre of shell. Carefully place white meat on either side.

Separate hard-boiled egg; sieve yolk and chop white. Cover dark meat with egg yolk, sprinkle a line of egg white on either side of this, then a line of parsley. Garnish with lemon slices and lettuce and serve with mayonnaise.

Serves 1.

CHEF'S SALAD

½ iceberg lettuce
½ Webb's lettuce
4 sticks celery, sliced
½ bunch radishes, sliced
185 g (6 oz) cold cooked chicken
125 g (4 oz) sliced ham
125 g (4 oz) Emmental cheese
BLUE CHEESE DRESSING:
3 tablespoons natural yogurt
3 tablespoons Mayonnaise
60 g (2 oz) Danish blue or Roquefort cheese, rinded and crumbled
1 teaspoon lemon juice

Shred iceberg lettuce, tear the Webb's into smaller pieces and put into a salad bowl with the celery and radishes. Cut the chicken, ham and cheese into strips and add to the salad.

To make the dressing, put ingredients into a blender or food processor and work until smooth. Pour over salad and toss gently to coat all the leaves.

Serves 4.

MARINATED BEEF SALAD

500 g (1 lb) piece rump steak
½ head Chinese leaves
1 large carrot
2 spring onions, thinly sliced
1 tomato, to garnish
TERIYAKI MARINADE:
6 tablespoons dry sherry
3 tablespoons soy sauce
1 tablespoon red wine vinegar
2 tablespoons clear honey
1 clove garlic, crushed
1 teaspoon ground ginger

To make the marinade, put all the ingredients into a bowl and mix together. Add beef, turn to coat with marinade. Cover and leave to marinate in the refrigerator overnight, turning meat once.

Preheat oven to 220C (425F/Gas 7). Drain the meat, put into an ovenproof dish, and cook in the oven for 25 minutes. Remove from oven, pour the juices into a jug, and leave to cool.

Arrange Chinese leaves on a platter. Place cooled meat, cut-side down on a board, slice downwards to give oval-shaped slices, then arrange these on the leaves. Skim fat from reserved cooking juices and discard. Drizzle juices over meat.

Using a potato peeler, cut thin ribbons from outside of carrot, discarding centre. Cut these ribbons into fine strips. Scatter the strips around the edge of the dish.

Scatter spring onions over the meat. With a sharp knife, cut peel from tomato and gently roll up to make a rose to garnish the centre of the salad.

Serves 4.

SAFFRON RICE RING

30 g (1 oz/6 teaspoons) butter
4 cardamom pods
3 cloves
5 cm (2 in) piece cinnamon stick
250 g (8 oz/1¼ cups) basmati rice
500 ml (16 fl oz/2 cups) hot chicken stock
good pinch saffron threads
125 g (4 oz) frozen petit pois
salt and pepper
3 tablespoons single (light) cream
mint sprigs and peeled prawns,
to garnish
FILLING:
250 g (8 oz) peeled cooked prawns
½ cucumber, diced
60 ml (2 fl oz/¼ cup) natural yogurt
2 teaspoons chopped fresh mint
pinch cayenne pepper

In a large saucepan, melt butter, add cardamoms, cloves and cinnamon stick and fry for 1 minute. Stir in rice and cook for 1 minute.

Gradually stir in hot chicken stock, keeping it simmering as it is added. Simmer rice for 15 minutes.

Meanwhile, put saffron into a cup, pour on 2 tablespoons hot water. Stir into rice with peas and continue to cook for 2 minutes. Remove from the heat and season to taste with salt and pepper.

Remove cardamoms, cloves and cinnamon stick, then stir in cream. Spoon rice into a 1.25 litre (2 pint/ 5 cup) ring mould, pressing down with the back of spoon. Cool, then refrigerate for 30 minutes.

Invert rice ring onto a plate. To make filling, mix all the ingredients together in a bowl, then spoon into centre of rice ring. Serve garnished with sprigs of mint and prawns.

Serves 4 as a main course or
6 as a side salad.

TONNO CON FAGIOLI

470 g (15 oz) can cannellini or borlotti beans, drained
440 g (14 oz) can flageolets (green kidney beans), drained
½ purple onion, sliced
salt and pepper
two 220 g (7 oz) cans tuna fish, drained
2 tablespoons chopped fresh parsley
black olives, lemon slices and parsley, to garnish
DRESSING:
75 ml (2½ fl oz/⅓ cup) virgin olive oil
1 tablespoon red wine vinegar

Put beans and flageolets into a bowl with onion and season with salt and pepper. Add tuna fish, breaking it into large flakes. Stir in parsley.

To make the dressing, put ingredients in a bowl or screw-top jar, mix well, then add to salad. Toss gently, then transfer to dish. Serve garnished with black olives, lemon slices and parsley.

Serves 4 as a main course and
6 as a starter.

MEDITERRANEAN LENTILS

250 g (8 oz/1¼ cups) brown or green lentils

250 g (8 oz) tomatoes, skinned, seeded and diced

3 sticks celery, sliced

125 g (4 oz) button mushrooms, sliced

celery leaves and lemon slices, to garnish

SPICY LEMON DRESSING:

75 ml (2½ fl oz/⅓ cup) virgin olive oil

1 tablespoon lemon juice

1 clove garlic, crushed

1 tablespoon chopped fresh parsley

½ teaspoon ground cumin

salt and pepper

Put the lentils in a sieve and rinse thoroughly, then tip into a saucepan and cover with water. Bring to the boil, then simmer for 30 minutes until tender. Drain and put into a bowl with the tomatoes, celery and mushrooms.

To make the dressing. Put all the ingredients in a bowl or screw-top jar and mix well. Pour over the salad and stir. Serve garnished with celery leaves and lemon slices.

Serves 6 as a side salad.

BULGAR MEDLEY

2 tablespoons sunflower oil

2 shallots, chopped

1 clove garlic, crushed

250 g (8 oz) bulgar wheat

500 ml (16 fl oz/2 cups) hot vegetable stock

2 carrots, diced

3 sticks celery, sliced

3 leeks, sliced

2 courgettes (zucchini), diced

fresh mint leaves, to garnish

GARLIC TOMATO DRESSING:

250 g (8 oz) tomatoes, skinned, seeded and finely chopped

3 tablespoons virgin olive oil

1 tablespoon wine vinegar

1 teaspoon tomato purée (paste)

1 clove garlic, crushed

½ teaspoon paprika

pinch sugar

salt and pepper

Heat oil in a saucepan, add shallots and garlic and cook for 2-3 minutes. Add bulgar wheat and stir for 1 minute over a medium heat. Gradually pour in hot stock and simmer for 5 minutes. Add carrots, celery and leeks and cook for 5 minutes. Stir in courgettes and cook for a further 2 minutes. Set aside.

To make the dressing, mix all the ingredients together in a bowl, then stir into bulgar salad. Leave to cool, then check the seasoning.

Serve garnished with fresh mint leaves.

Serves 6-8 as a side salad.

Variation: Other lightly cooked vegetables can be substituted for the ones used here.

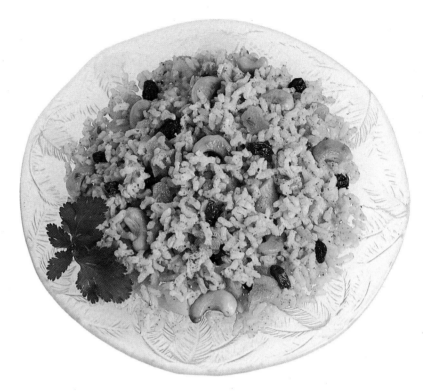

BUTTER BEAN SALAD

250 g (8 oz) dried butter beans, soaked
overnight
salt
185 g (6 oz) streaky bacon, rinds removed
snipped chives, to garnish
TOMATO DRESSING:
185 g (6 oz) tomatoes, skinned, seeded and
chopped
1 teaspoon tomato purée (paste)
3 tablespoons extra virgin olive oil
2 teaspoons lemon juice
salt and pepper

Rinse butter beans, put into a
saucepan, cover with water and
simmer for about 1 hour until

tender. Add salt during last 5
minutes of cooking.

Meanwhile, cook bacon in a frying pan until crisp. Remove from
the pan and drain on absorbent
kitchen paper, then crumble into
small pieces.

To make the dressing, put all the
ingredients into a blender and work
until tomatoes are pulpy. Drain
beans, put into a serving dish and
pour over the dressing. Mix in
bacon. Leave to cool. Serve garnished with snipped chives.

Serves 4-6 as a side salad.

CURRIED RICE SALAD

90 g (3 oz) semi-dried apricots, chopped
250 g (8 oz/1⅓ cups) long grain brown rice
3 tablespoons sunflower oil
60 g (2 oz/⅓ cup) cashew nuts
1 onion, chopped
1 teaspoon cumin seeds
3 teaspoons curry powder
90 ml (3 fl oz/⅓ cup) orange juice
60 g (2 oz/⅓ cup) raisins
salt and pepper
coriander sprigs, to garnish

Put chopped apricots in a bowl,
pour over sufficient boiling water to
cover and leave to soak for 45
minutes.

Meanwhile, cook rice in boiling
salted water for 40 minutes until
tender.

Heat the oil in a frying pan, add
cashew nuts and fry until golden.

Remove with a slotted spoon and
drain on absorbent kitchen paper.
Add onion to pan and cook over a
medium heat for 3-4 minutes. Stir
in cumin seeds and curry powder
and cook for 2 minutes. Pour in
orange juice and simmer for 1
minute. Remove from heat.

Drain rice, rinse under cold run-
ning water, then drain again. Put
into a large bowl, add the warm
curry sauce and mix well.

Drain apricots and stir into rice
with nuts and raisins. Season with
salt and pepper. Allow the salad to
stand for at least 2 hours before
serving to allow flavours to mingle.
Serve garnished with sprigs of fresh
coriander.

Serves 6 as a side salad.

MEXICAN BEAN SALAD

440 g (14 oz) can red kidney beans, drained

185 g (6 oz) frozen sweetcorn, cooked

1 green pepper (capsicum), seeded and chopped

½ bunch spring onions, chopped

2 tablespoons chopped fresh coriander

½ iceberg lettuce, shredded, if desired

lime slices and parsley sprigs, to garnish

LIME DRESSING:

60 ml (2 fl oz/¼ cup) virgin olive oil

juice of ½ lime

1 clove garlic, crushed

salt and pepper

Put the kidney beans, sweetcorn, green pepper (capsicum), spring onions and coriander into a bowl.

To make the dressing, put all the ingredients into a bowl or screw-top jar and mix well. Pour over the salad and toss together.

Line a serving dish with the shredded iceberg lettuce, if desired, and spoon the bean mixture on top. Serve the salad garnished with lime slices and sprigs of parsley.

Serves 4-6 as a side salad.

TABBOULEH

185 g (6 oz) bulgar wheat

60 ml (2 fl oz/¼ cup) lemon juice

60 ml (2 fl oz/¼ cup) virgin olive oil

1 tablespoon finely chopped Spanish onion

6 spring onions, finely chopped

90 g (3 oz) bunch flat leaf parsley, chopped

30 g (1 oz) fresh mint, chopped

salt and pepper

1 cos lettuce

cherry tomatoes and parsley sprigs, to garnish

Put bulgar into a bowl, cover with warm water and leave to soak for 30 minutes. Squeeze out excess water and put bulgar into a bowl. Add lemon juice, oil, onion, spring onions, parsley and mint and season to taste with salt and pepper. Mix together, then chill for a least 1 hour.

To serve, arrange cos lettuce leaves around the edge of a platter, spoon salad in the centre and garnish with cherry tomatoes and sprigs of parsley.

Serves 6.

SPICED CHICK-PEA SALAD

JAPANESE VINEGARED SALAD

375 g (12 oz/2 cups) dried chick-peas, soaked overnight

2 tablespoons chopped fresh coriander and coriander sprigs, to garnish

CORIANDER DRESSING:

3 tablespoons olive oil

1 small onion, chopped

1 green chilli, seeded and finely chopped

1 clove garlic, finely chopped

2 teaspoons ground coriander

1 teaspoon ground cumin

1 teaspoon turmeric

salt and pepper

2 tablespoons natural yogurt

Drain chick-peas from soaking water and put into a saucepan with fresh water. Bring to the boil, and simmer for 1 hour or until tender.

Meanwhile, make the dressing. Heat oil in a small frying pan, add onion, chilli and garlic and cook for 2-3 minutes. Stir in spices and cook for 1 minute. Season to taste with salt and pepper. Turn into a large bowl and stir in the yogurt.

Drain chick-peas, cool briefly then remove skins while still warm. Add to spice mixture and mix well. Leave to marinate for at least 2 hours. Serve garnished with the coriander.

Serves 6 as a side salad.

125 g (4 oz) mange tout (snow peas), trimmed

185 g (6 oz/1 cup) long grain rice

JAPANESE DRESSING:

2 tablespoons rice vinegar

1 tablespoon light sesame oil

1 teaspoon dark sesame oil

4 teaspoons tamari (Japanese soy sauce)

4 spring onions, chopped

Blanch the mange tout (snow peas) in a saucepan of boiling water for 30 seconds, drain, rinse under cold water, then dry on absorbent kitchen paper. Arrange around edge of serving dish.

Cook rice in boiling salted water for 10-12 minutes until tender. Drain, rinse with cold water, then drain again. Put rice into a bowl. To make the dressing, mix ingredients together in a bowl or screw-top jar. Stir into rice. Spoon rice into serving dish and serve.

Serves 4-6.

Variation: The dressed rice can be wrapped in small blanched spinach or vine leaves. Cut the parcels in half, then stand them on end to resemble Japanese sushi.

HUMMUS SALAD

470 g (15 oz) can chick-peas, drained

60 ml (2 fl oz/¼ cup) virgin olive oil

3 tablespoons tahini (sesame seed paste)

2 cloves garlic

juice of 1 lemon

salt and pepper

1 teaspoon paprika

olives and coriander leaves, to garnish

TO SERVE:

carrot sticks or baby carrots

celery sticks

radishes

Put chick-peas in a blender or food processor with 3 tablespoons of oil, tahini, garlic and lemon juice. Work until smooth, then season.

Spoon into a serving bowl or 4 individual dishes. Drizzle remaining oil over and dust with paprika.

Garnish and serve with the raw fresh vegetables.

Serves 4 as a starter or light meal.

THREE BEAN SALAD

125 g (4 oz) dried red kidney beans, soaked overnight

salt and pepper

185 g (6 oz) thin green beans, trimmed and cut into 4 cm (1½ in) lengths

250 g (8 oz) shelled broad beans

shallot rings, to garnish

SHALLOT DRESSING:

60 ml (2 fl oz/¼ cup) virgin olive oil

1 tablespoon red wine vinegar

1 shallot, finely chopped

Put red kidney beans into a saucepan with water to cover and boil for 1½ hours until tender, adding salt 5 minutes before the end of the cooking time. Drain, put into a bowl, and leave to cool.

Cook green beans and broad beans in boiling salted water for about 5 minutes until just tender. Drain, skin broad beans, and add both beans to the kidney beans.

To make the dressing, mix ingredients together in a bowl or screw-top jar, seasoning to taste with salt and pepper. Pour over the salad and toss. Transfer to a serving dish, cover and refrigerate until required. Serve garnished with shallot rings.

Serves 4-6.

THOUSAND ISLAND SALAD

750 g (1½ lb) firm white fish, such as bass, cod, halibut, swordfish, monkfish

juice of 1 lemon

salt and pepper

2 kiwi fruit

2 tamarillos

1 small mango

paprika and parsley sprigs, to garnish

THOUSAND ISLAND DRESSING:

1 quantity Mayonnaise

1 teaspoon tomato purée (paste)

3 teaspoons lemon juice

6 stuffed olives, chopped

2 spring onions, finely chopped

1 tablespoon chopped fresh parsley

1 hard-boiled egg, chopped

½ teaspoon paprika

½ teaspoon sugar

Preheat oven to 190C (375F/Gas 5). Skin the fish and put into an ovenproof dish, sprinkle over lemon juice and season with salt and pepper. Cook in the oven for 15-20 minutes. Allow to cool, then cut into cubes. Spoon over a little of the cooking juices to keep the fish moist.

Meanwhile, make the dressing by mixing all the ingredients together in a bowl.

Prepare the fruit. Peel the kiwi fruit and tamarillos, then slice. Peel the mango and cut into sticks.

Divide the fish between 4 plates, arrange the tropical fruits around the fish, then either spoon over the dressing or serve it on one side. Garnish fish with a little paprika and sprigs of parsley.

Serves 4 as a main course.

GINGER PORK & LYCHEES

2 tablespoons light sesame oil

500 g (1 lb) pork fillet, cut into strips

1 clove garlic, crushed

1 tablespoon chopped fresh ginger

90 g (3 oz) mange tout (snow peas), cut into thin strips

470 g (15 oz) can lychees, drained

½ head Chinese leaves

chilli flowers, to garnish

SWEET AND SOUR DRESSING:

2 tablespoons light sesame oil

4 teaspoons rice vinegar

2 teaspoons dark soy sauce

1 teaspoon honey

1 teaspoon tomato purée (paste)

Heat oil in a large frying pan or wok, add pork, garlic and ginger and cook until pork is lightly browned. Add mange tout (snow peas) and cook for 30 seconds. Remove from heat, transfer with a slotted spoon, and add lychees.

To make the dressing, mix ingredients together in a bowl. Pour over salad, then leave to cool.

Shred Chinese leaves, arrange on serving platter or dishes. Spoon salad on top, garnish and serve.

Serves 4 as a main course.

CHICKEN & GRAPE SALAD

500 g (1 lb) cooked cold chicken, cut into small dice
3 sticks celery, chopped
125 g (4 oz) black grapes
125 g (4 oz) green grapes
½ lettuce, finely shredded, if desired
nasturtium flowers and tarragon sprigs, to garnish
TARRAGON CREAM DRESSING:
3 tablespoons virgin olive oil
1 tablespoon tarragon vinegar
3 tablespoons thick sour cream
salt and pepper

Put chicken and celery in a bowl. Halve grapes, remove pips and add to the bowl.

To make the dressing, mix all the ingredients together in a bowl or screw-top jar. Pour over salad and toss together. Divide lettuce, if using, between 4 plates and spoon chicken salad on top. Serve garnished with nasturtium flowers and tarragon.

Serves 4 as a main course.

ROLLMOP & APPLE SALAD

8 rollmop herrings
2 green eating apples
2 tablespoons lemon juice
1 bulb fennel, finely sliced
hard-boiled egg slices and dill sprigs, to garnish
SOUR CREAM DILL DRESSING:
155 ml (5 fl oz/⅔ cup) carton thick sour cream
2 tablespoons natural yogurt
2 teaspoons creamed horseradish sauce
1 tablespoon chopped fresh dill
salt and pepper

Cut rollmops into bite-sized pieces and put into a bowl. Core and chop apples, put into a second bowl with lemon juice; toss to prevent discolouration. Remove apple and add to the herrings with the fennel.

To make the dressing, mix ingredients together in a bowl, then stir into the salad. Transfer to a serving dish and serve garnished with slices of hard-boiled egg and sprigs of dill.

Serves 4 as a main course.

CHEESE & FRUIT PLATTER

2 green eating apples

juice of ½ lemon

125 g (4 oz) smoked cheese, cubed

250 g (8 oz) brie, or 1 whole camembert, sliced

4 sticks celery, sliced

185 g (6 oz) grapes

celery leaves or mustard and cress, to garnish

LEMON MAYONNAISE:

½ quantity Mayonnaise

½ teaspoon finely grated lemon peel

2 teaspoons lemon juice

Quarter and core the apples, then slice and place in a bowl with the lemon juice. Stir to coat. Arrange cubed and sliced the cheese and the apple slices on 4 plates.

Make an attractive pattern with the celery and grapes. Garnish with celery leaves or mustard and cress. To make the mayonnaise, mix all the ingredients together in a bowl. Serve the mayonnaise separately.

Serves 4.

TURKEY & CRANBERRY SALAD

500 g (1 lb) turkey escalopes

2 tablespoons virgin olive oil

1 small onion, chopped

125 g (4 oz) fresh or frozen cranberries

grated peel of ½ orange

orange slices and watercress sprigs, to garnish

MARINADE:

juice of 1 lime

125 ml (4 fl oz/½ cup) dry vermouth

2 teaspoons clear honey

½ teaspoon dry oregano

salt and pepper

Cut the turkey escalopes into thin strips. Mix marinade ingredients together in a bowl. Add turkey strips and marinate for 2 hours.

Remove turkey from marinade with a slotted spoon; reserve marinade. Heat oil in a frying pan, add turkey and onion and sauté for 5 minutes. Pour reserved marinade into the pan with the cranberries and orange peel and cook gently until the cranberries begin to split. Transfer the mixture to a dish to cool.

Stir the salad and spoon into a serving dish. Serve garnished with orange slices and sprigs of watercress.

Serves 3-4 as a main course.

CHICORY & ORANGE SALAD

60 g (2 oz/⅓ cup) hazelnuts

4 heads chicory, chopped

3 oranges

1 tablespoon chopped fresh parsley

HAZELNUT DRESSING:

3 tablespoons hazelnut oil

3 tablespoons orange juice

pinch mixed spice

salt and pepper

Place hazelnuts on baking sheet and brown under a hot grill until the skins begin to crack. Allow to cool a little, then rub off the skins. Roughly chop the nuts. Put chicory in a large bowl.

Cut peel and pith from oranges. Holding each one over a bowl to catch juice, cut into segments. Cut the segments in half and add to the chicory.

To make the dressing, add all the ingredients to the juice in a bowl, mix well, then pour over the salad. Toss gently, then transfer to a serving dish. Scatter over the hazelnuts and serve garnished with chopped parsley.

Serves 4-6 as a side salad.

AVOCADO & CITRUS SALAD

½ curly endive, torn into pieces

2 oranges

1 grapefruit

1 ripe avocado

CITRUS DRESSING:

3 teaspoons sunflower oil

peel and juice of ½ lime

1 tablespoon chopped fresh mint

salt and pepper

Put endive into a salad bowl. Cut peel and pith from oranges and grapefruit. Holding each one over a bowl to catch juice, remove segments and halve. Arrange on top of endive.

Halve avocado, remove stone, slice or dice flesh, then add to salad.

To make the dressing, mix all the ingredients in a bowl or screw-top jar with 2 tablespoons of juice. Spoon over salad, and serve.

Serves 4 as a side salad.

PERSIAN CARROT SALAD

500 g (1 lb) carrots, grated
2 large oranges
90 g (3 oz/½ cup) raisins
60 g (2 oz/⅓ cup) blanched almonds, lightly toasted
lime slices, to garnish
SPICY DRESSING:
2 tablespoons virgin olive oil
2 tablespoons lime juice
1 teaspoon ground cumin
½ teaspoon ground cinnamon
½ teaspoon caster sugar

Put carrots into a bowl. Cut peel and pith from oranges. Remove segments and chop. Add to carrots with raisins and almonds.

To make the dressing, mix all the ingredients together in a bowl or screw-top jar. Add to salad. Toss together, then refrigerate for 1 hour. Serve garnished with lime slices.

Serves 6 as a side salad.

ASPARAGUS & AVOCADO SALAD

500 g (1 lb) asparagus spears
1 ripe avocado
4 teaspoons chopped pistachio nuts or walnuts
fennel sprigs and orange segments, to garnish
MARINADE:
125 ml (4 fl oz/½ cup) walnut oil
6 teaspoons freshly squeezed orange juice
2 teaspoons grated orange peel
2 teaspoons light soft brown sugar
½ teaspoon salt
½ teaspoon black pepper
2 teaspoons Dijon mustard
6 teaspoons chopped fresh fennel

Trim asparagus spears and, using a sharp knife, peel outside skin off each stem. Cook asparagus in large shallow saucepan of boiling salted water for 5-8 minutes, until tender. Drain and cool.

To make marinade, mix oil, orange juice, peel, sugar, salt, pepper, mustard and fennel together, stirring until well blended.

Place asparagus spears in a shallow dish, pour over marinade and turn each spear in marinade to coat evenly. Cover with plastic wrap and leave in a cool place for 1 hour or until ready to serve.

Lift out asparagus and arrange on 4 individual serving plates. Peel and dice avocado and add to marinade with pistachios or walnuts, turning gently.

Spoon avocado and nut mixture over centres of asparagus spears and garnish with sprigs of fennel and orange segments.

Serves 4.

FRUITY COLESLAW

375 g (12 oz) white or light green cabbage, finely shredded

440 g (14 oz) can pineapple slices or 375 g (12 oz) fresh pineapple, chopped

1½ eating apples

2 teaspoons lemon juice

90 g (3 oz/½ cup) raisins

60 g (2 oz/⅓ cup) salted peanuts

½ apple, sliced, or pineapple leaves to garnish

DRESSING:

1 quantity Mayonnaise

1 teaspoon clear honey

3 tablespoons pineapple or apple juice

salt and pepper

Put cabbage into a large bowl. If using canned pineapple, drain well, reserving the juice, and chop the fruit. Add pineapple to cabbage.

Core and chop apples, toss in lemon juice and add to salad with raisins and peanuts.

To make the dressing, mix all the ingredients in a bowl, using reserved pineapple juice or apple juice, then pour over the salad. Mix well, then turn into a serving dish. Garnish and serve at once.

Serves 6-8 as a side salad.

APPLE & CELERIAC SALAD

1 celeriac

3 eating apples

2 tablespoons lemon juice

POPPY SEED DRESSING:

2 tablespoons poppy seeds

60 g (2 oz/¼ cup) thick natural yogurt

3 tablespoons apple juice

salt and pepper

Peel celeriac; cut into 1 cm (½ in) thick slices. Put into a saucepan of boiling water and simmer for 7-8 minutes until just tender. Drain and leave to cool.

Cut apples into quarters; remove cores. Slice 4 quarters; dice remainder. Put all the apple into a bowl with lemon juice and toss together.

Remove apple slices, put to one side for garnishing. Dice the celeriac and mix with the diced apples.

To make the dressing, mix all the ingredients together in a screw-top jar, then pour over the salad and toss together. Transfer to a serving dish and serve garnished with apple slices.

Serves 6 as a side salad.

CLASSIC TOMATO SALAD

500 g (1 lb) firm tomatoes
1 teaspoon sugar
salt and pepper
90 ml (3 fl oz/⅓ cup) virgin olive oil
2 tablespoons white wine vinegar
1 tablespoon snipped chives
chopped mixed fresh herbs, to garnish

Slice tomatoes thinly and arrange on a serving plate. Sprinkle with sugar and season with salt and pepper. Mix oil and vinegar together in a bowl or screw-top jar, then spoon over the salad.

Scatter over chives, then cover salad and refrigerate for a least 1 hour before serving. Garnish with mixed herbs.

Serves 4-6.

Variation: Sprinkle tomatoes with finely chopped spring onion or shredded basil instead of chives.

GERMAN POTATO SALAD

1 kg (2 lb) potatoes, scrubbed
6 spring onions, finely chopped
salt and pepper
3 tablespoons Mayonnaise
3 tablespoons natural yogurt
snipped chives, to garnish

Cook unpeeled potatoes in a saucepan of boiling salted water for about 15 minutes until tender.

Drain, then cool a little before removing skins. Cool completely. Dice potatoes and put into a bowl with spring onions, then season with salt and pepper.

Mix mayonnaise and yogurt together in a bowl, then fold into the salad. Spoon into serving dish and serve garnished with chives.

Serves 6.

Note: The potato skins can be left on if preferred.

COLESLAW

500 g (1 lb) white cabbage, shredded

2 carrots, coarsely grated

5 sticks celery, sliced

2 tablespoons chopped fresh parsley

celery leaves, to garnish

BOILED DRESSING:

2 tablespoons sunflower oil

3 teaspoons flour

2 teaspoons vinegar

1 teaspoon dry mustard

1 egg, beaten

salt and pepper

pinch cayenne pepper

Put cabbage, carrots, celery and parsley into a bowl and mix well.

To make the dressing, blend oil and flour in a saucepan, add 125 ml (4 fl oz/½ cup) water, the vinegar, mustard, egg and seasonings. Cook over a very low heat until thickened, stirring all the time. Cool slightly, then pour over the salad and mix well. Cool before serving garnished with celery leaves.

Serves 6-8.

GREEK SALAD

½ cos lettuce, chopped

a few young spinach leaves, shredded

3 tomatoes, cut into wedges

½ cucumber, halved lengthwise and sliced

½ Spanish onion, cut into rings

1 green pepper (capsicum), seeded and sliced

185 g (6 oz) feta cheese, cubed

12 black olives

1 teaspoon chopped fresh oregano

LEMON DRESSING:

60 ml (2 fl oz/¼ cup) extra virgin olive oil

1 tablespoon lemon juice

salt and pepper

Put lettuce, spinach, tomatoes, cucumber, onion and pepper (capsicum) into a bowl. Top with cheese and olives; sprinkle with oregano.

Mix dressing ingredients. Spoon over the salad and serve.

Serves 4.

CAULIFLOWER SALAD

1 cauliflower
1 bunch radishes, trimmed and sliced
toasted sesame seeds
radishes, to garnish
TAHINI DRESSING:
155 ml (5 fl oz/⅔ cup) natural yogurt
4 teaspoons tahini (sesame seed paste)
1 teaspoon clear honey

Break cauliflower into small flowerets, blanch in a saucepan of boiling water for 2 minutes, drain and cool. Put into a bowl with radishes.

To make the dressing, mix all the ingredients together in a bowl. Pour onto salad and mix well. Spoon into a serving dish and sprinkle with sesame seeds. Serve garnished with radishes.

Serves 6.

FRENCH POTATO SALAD

750 g (1½ lb) new potatoes, scrubbed
1 tablespoon virgin olive oil
2 tablespoons chopped mixed herbs and herb sprigs
HERB VINAIGRETTE:
3 tablespoons virgin olive oil
1 tablespoon white wine vinegar
salt and pepper

Boil unpeeled potatoes in a saucepan of salted water for about 15 minutes until tender. Drain. If they are small leave whole, otherwise cool a little, then cut into slices, halves or quarters. Put into a bowl and, while still warm, pour over 1 tablespoon oil. Leave to cool.

To make the dressing, mix together oil and vinegar in a bowl or screw-top jar. Season with salt and pepper, then stir into potatoes. Just before serving, sprinkle with chopped herbs and gently fold in. Garnish with sprigs of herbs.

Serves 4-6.

COURGETTE SALAD

500 g (1 lb) courgettes (zucchini),
coarsely grated

salt

fresh herbs or baby courgettes (zucchini)
and flowers, to garnish

HERB YOGURT MAYONNAISE:

2 tablespoons Mayonnaise

2 teaspoons chopped fresh parsley

2 teaspoons chopped fresh tarragon

2 teaspoons chopped fresh chervil

2 teaspoons chopped fresh chives

60 ml (2 fl oz / ¼ cup) natural yogurt

pepper

Place courgettes (zucchini) on 3 layers of absorbent kitchen paper, sprinkle with salt and leave for 1 hour.

To make the dressing, mix all the ingredients together in a large bowl. Add courgettes (zucchini) to dressing and stir together. Spoon into a serving dish and serve garnished with fresh herbs or baby courgettes (zucchini) and flowers.

Serves 6.

TRICOLOUR PASTA SALAD

250 g (8 oz) tricoloured pasta twists

salt

1 tablespoon virgin olive oil

125 g (4 oz) open-caped mushrooms,
sliced (use wild mushrooms
if available)

90 g (3 oz) green olives, stoned and
chopped

60 g (2 oz) can anchovies, drained and cut
into thin strips

1 tablespoon chopped fresh oregano

oregano sprigs, to garnish

DRESSING:

2 tablespoons virgin olive oil

1 tablespoon balsamico vinegar

pepper

Cook pasta in boiling salted water for 5-6 minutes until just tender, then drain and rinse under cold water and drain again.

Heat the oil in a frying pan and cook the mushrooms for 2-3 minutes. Cool, then put into a bowl with the cooked pasta, olives, anchovies and oregano.

To make the dressing, mix together the oil and vinegar and season with pepper. Pour over the salad and toss together. Serve garnished with sprigs of oregano.

Serves 4-6.

SWEET PEPPER SALAD

2 large red peppers (capsicums)
2 large yellow peppers (capsicums)
90 ml (3 fl oz/⅓ cup) extra virgin olive oil
2 cloves garlic
salt and pepper
black olives and fresh parsley, to garnish

Put peppers (capsicums) under a hot grill, turning them until skins are blistered and black all over. Place in a polythene bag and leave to cool for 10-15 minutes. Peel skins off, remove stems and seeds and cut flesh into strips. Arrange in a shallow dish.

Drizzle olive oil over peppers. Peel garlic, cut into slivers and scatter over peppers. Season with salt and pepper, then leave to marinate for 24 hours.

Serve garnished with black olives and parsley.

Serves 4-6.

SUMMER RATATOUILLE

60 ml (2 fl oz/¼ cup) virgin olive oil
1 bulb fennel, sliced
1 large onion, sliced
1 clove garlic, crushed
1 large beefsteak tomato, peeled and chopped
1 red pepper (capsicum), seeded
1 yellow pepper (capsicum), seeded
1 green pepper (capsicum), seeded
375 g (12 oz) courgettes (zucchini), sliced
1 teaspoon chopped fresh thyme
salt and pepper
shredded basil leaves and fennel fronds, to garnish

Heat oil in a large saucepan, add fennel, onion and garlic, cover and cook gently for 5 minutes. Add tomato; cook for 10 minutes.

Cut peppers (capsicums) into squares, add to pan with courgettes (zucchini) and thyme. Season with salt and pepper and cook for a further 5 minutes. Leave to cool.

Spoon the salad into a serving dish and serve garnished with basil leaves and fennel fronds.

Serves 6.

MOROCCAN SUGARED LETTUCE

1 crisp, curly-leaf lettuce, such as Webb's, escarole or batavia
125 g (4 oz) fresh dates, halved and stoned
3 satsumas or clementines
2 tablespoons caster sugar
3 tablespoons white wine vinegar
pepper

Shred lettuce, then put into salad bowl with the dates.

With a zester, peel shreds of peel from one satsuma or clementine; reserve. Remove peel and pith from fruit, then cut fruit into slices. Break slices into smaller pieces and add to bowl. Sprinkle over sugar and toss salad, then sprinkle over vinegar and toss again. Season with pepper and serve garnished with reserved shreds of peel.

Serves 6.

RADISH SALAD

1 mouli (white radish), weighing about 250 g (8 oz)
salt
1 bunch radishes, trimmed and quartered
1 tablespoon sesame seeds
radish leaves, to garnish
SESAME VINAIGRETTE:
1 tablespoon sunflower oil
1 teaspoon dark sesame oil
2 teaspoons rice vinegar

Grate mouli (white radish) or cut into matchstick strips, place on absorbent kitchen paper and sprinkle with salt. Leave for 30 minutes. Squeeze out any excess moisture, then put mouli (white radish) into a bowl and mix with radishes.

To make the dressing, mix all the ingredients together in a bowl or screw-top jar, then stir into the salad. Spoon salad into a serving dish and serve sprinkled with sesame seeds and garnished with radish leaves.

Serves 6.

CUCUMBER & DILL SALAD

1 large cucumber
salt
4 teaspoons lemon juice or white wine vinegar
black pepper, if desired
1 tablespoon chopped fresh dill

Peel cucumber, reserving a few strips of peel. Cut cucumber in half lengthwise and hollow out the seeds with a teaspoon. Slice thinly, then put into a colander, sprinkle with salt and leave to drain for 30 minutes. Rinse with cold water and dry on absorbent paper.

Put cucumber into a bowl and sprinkle with lemon juice or vinegar. Season with pepper, if desired, then stir in dill and serve garnished with strips of cucumber peel.

Serves 4-6.

ARRANGED GREEN SALAD

90 g (3 oz) mange tout (snow peas)
250 g (8 oz) fresh asparagus, trimmed
2 avocados
watercress sprigs and alfalfa sprouts, to garnish
LIME AND PISTACHIO DRESSING:
grated peel and juice of ½ lime
1 tablespoon virgin olive oil
1 tablespoon sunflower oil
30 g (1 oz) shelled pistachio nuts
salt and pepper

Blanch mange tout (snow peas) in a saucepan of boiling water for 30 seconds, drain and dry on absorbent kitchen paper. Cook asparagus in boiling water for 7-8 minutes until tender, then drain and cool.

Halve avocados, remove stones and peel. Place, cut side down, on a chopping board and slice crosswise. Gently separate slices and transfer to 4 plates.

Arrange mange tout (snow peas) and asparagus down either side of avocado. To make the dressing, mix all the ingredients together in a bowl or screw-top jar, then spoon over the salad. Garnish with watercress sprigs and alfalfa sprouts.

Serves 4.

HERB CUCUMBER FRAIS

1 cucumber
250 g (8 oz/1 cup) fromage frais
dill sprigs and chive flowers, to garnish
MARINADE:
4 teaspoons chopped fresh tarragon
4 teaspoons chopped fresh dill
4 teaspoons snipped fresh chives
½ teaspoon salt
½ teaspoon black pepper
½ teaspoon dry mustard
6 teaspoons red vermouth

Using a canelle cutter, cut off thin strips of cucumber peel to make a ridge effect. Cut cucumber in half lengthwise, scoop out seeds and cut cucumber into 0.5 cm (¼ in) slices.

Bring 155 ml (5 fl oz/⅔ cup) water to boil in a pan, add cucumber and cook for 1 minute. Drain.

To make marinade, mix tarragon, dill, chives, salt, pepper, mustard and vermouth together. Add cucumber and turn gently in marinade to coat. Cover with plastic wrap and leave in a cool place for 2 hours.

Just before serving, gently stir in fromage frais until evenly mixed. Place cucumber mixture in a serving dish and garnish with sprigs of dill and chive flowers.

Serves 4.

TOSSED GREEN SALAD

mixture of lettuce to include 2 varieties, such as cos, Webb's, iceberg, Little Gem, endive or batavia
a few young spinach leaves
1 bunch watercress, trimmed
½ cucumber, sliced or diced
1 green pepper (capsicum), seeded and chopped
2 tablespoons chopped mixed fresh herbs, such as parsley, chervil, tarragon, summer savory or chives
DRESSING:
1 clove garlic
salt
1 tablespoon wine vinegar
2 teaspoons lemon juice
¼ teaspoon Dijon mustard
60 ml (2 fl oz/¼ cup) extra virgin olive oil

Tear salad and spinach leaves into smaller pieces. If not using immediately, place in a polythene bag in the refrigerator.

Make the dressing in a wooden salad bowl. Put garlic and a little salt into bowl and crush to a paste with back of a wooden spoon. Add vinegar, lemon juice and mustard, then stir in oil; continue to mix to make an emulsion.

Add all the salad ingredients to the bowl, toss well so that every leaf is coated with dressing. Serve immediately.

Serves 6 as a side salad.

Note: For a less garlicky flavour, rub the inside of the bowl with a cut clove of garlic, then discard.

If you do not have a wooden salad bowl, the dressing can be made separately and poured over just before serving.

CALIFORNIAN SALAD

6 teaspoons powdered gelatine
4 teaspoons sugar
2 lemons
3 tablespoons wine vinegar
few drops yellow food colouring
250 g (8 oz) fresh asparagus, cooked
1 large avocado
2 large carrots, grated
fresh herbs, to garnish

Sprinkle gelatine over 90 ml (3 fl oz/ ⅓ cup) water in a small bowl and leave to soften for 2-3 minutes. Stand bowl in a saucepan of hot water and stir until dissolved. Stir in sugar, then set aside to cool.

Grate the peel from 1 of the lemons and squeeze the juice from both. Reserve 1 tablespoon lemon juice. Put the grated peel and remaining juice into a measuring jug and make up to 940 ml (30 fl oz/ 3¾ cups) with water. Add dissolved gelatine, the vinegar and a few drops of yellow food colouring. Pour a little of the liquid into a 1.8 litre (3 pint/7½ cup) ring mould and refrigerate until the jelly has set.

Cut the tips off the asparagus and arrange on the set jelly. Halve avocado, remove stone, peel, then dice flesh. Place in a bowl and mix with reserved lemon juice. Chop asparagus stalks and add to the avocado with the carrots. Mix well. Stir in remaining liquid, then spoon into the mould. Refrigerate until set.

To serve, turn out the vegetable ring onto a plate and garnish with herbs.

Serves 8.

SUNSHINE SALAD

375 g (12 oz) carrots, cut into matchstick strips
1 yellow pepper (capsicum), seeded and cut into thin strips
1 red pepper (capsicum), seeded and cut into thin strips
125 g (4 oz) frozen sweetcorn, cooked
1 tablespoon sunflower seeds
LEMON MUSTARD VINAIGRETTE:
60 ml (2 fl oz/¼ cup) sunflower oil
5 teaspoons lemon juice
½ teaspoon Dijon mustard
salt and pepper

Arrange strips of carrot round the outer edge of a shallow bowl or plate. Place the pepper (capsicum) strips inside this ring in alternate groups. Spoon the sweetcorn into the centre.

To make the dressing, mix all the ingredients together in a bowl or screw-top jar, then drizzle over the salad. Sprinkle with sunflower seeds just before serving.

Serves 6-8.

FENNEL SALAD

CUCUMBER RAITA

12 radishes
3 fennel bulbs
2 carrots
1 green eating apple
1 tablespoon lemon juice
6 tablespoons mayonnaise

1 small cucumber
1 teaspoon salt
625 ml (20 fl oz/2½ cups) natural yogurt
1 teaspoon finely chopped onion
1 teaspoon chopped fresh coriander leaves
pepper
coriander leaves, to garnish

Trim radishes and make vertical cuts on 4 sides. Soak in ice cold water for 2-3 hours until 'petals' open. Drain and reserve for garnish.

Peel cucumber and chop finely. Put into a nylon sieve, resting on a thick fold of absorbent kitchen paper. Sprinkle with salt and leave for 1 hour for moisture in cucumber to drain away.

Trim fennel and reserve fern-like tops for garnish. Cut bulbs in half, discarding any hard core. Slice thinly. Peel carrots and cut into thin matchstick strips. Core and dice unpeeled apple. Mix lemon juice into vegetables, then stir in mayonnaise.

Line another sieve with muslin, place over a bowl and pour in yogurt. Leave in a cool place for 2 hours.

Turn mixed ingredients into a salad bowl and garnish with radish flowers and fennel tops.

Serves 4-6.

Note: Fennel has a strong aniseed flavour and goes particularly well with fish.

Discard the whey and mix drained yogurt, cucumber, onion and chopped coriander leaves together. Season to taste with pepper. Transfer to a bowl and garnish with coriander leaves.

Makes 500 ml (16 fl oz/2 cups).

SANDWICHES

CUCUMBER-MINT COOLERS

¼ cucumber, peeled and thinly sliced

½ teaspoon salt

2 teaspoons finely chopped fresh mint

good pinch caster sugar

¼ teaspoon lemon juice

45 g (1½ oz/9 teaspoons) butter, softened

4 thin slices brown or white bread from a small loaf, crusts removed

pepper

mint sprigs, to garnish

Put the cucumber into a sieve and sprinkle with salt, then press down with a saucer and leave to drain for 30 minutes.

Meanwhile, in a bowl, mix mint with sugar, lemon juice and butter until soft and creamy. Butter the slices of bread.

Pat cucumber dry on absorbent kitchen paper and arrange over 2 slices of buttered bread. Season with pepper. Cover with remaining bread slices and press together.

Cut into dainty squares or fingers. Arrange on a serving plate, garnished with sprigs of mint.

Makes 8.

Note: For special occasions, cut sandwiches into dainty shapes using a selection of biscuit cutters.

SALMON PINWHEELS

1 large unsliced white sandwich loaf, crusts removed

90 g (3 oz/⅓ cup) butter, softened

3 tablespoons finely chopped fresh parsley

1 teaspoon lemon juice

good pinch cayenne pepper

125 g (4 oz) thinly sliced smoked salmon

pepper

lemon twists, to garnish

Carefully cut two 0.5 cm (¼ in) thick lengthwise slices from the sandwich loaf. Using a rolling pin, roll each slice firmly to flatten.

In a bowl, mix butter with 1 tablespoon parsley, lemon juice and cayenne pepper until well combined. Spread two-thirds of the butter mixture over the slices of bread, reserving a little for later.

Arrange smoked salmon on top of buttered bread and season with pepper. Roll up each slice, like a Swiss roll, starting from a short side.

Spread remaining butter all over outside of rolls and coat evenly in remaining chopped parsley.

Wrap rolls tightly in plastic film and chill for at least 2 hours. Remove plastic film and cut each roll into 7 pinwheels. Arrange on a serving plate, garnished with lemon twists.

Makes 14.

Variation: Coat one whole buttered roll with chopped parsley and the remaining buttered roll in paprika. Chill as above before cutting into pinwheels. Attractively arrange the different rolls on a serving plate.

LOBSTER SANDWICHES

185 g (6 oz) cooked lobster, thawed if frozen and chopped
2 small sticks celery, finely chopped
3 tablespoons mayonnaise
salt
cayenne pepper
60 g (2 oz ¼ cup) butter, softened
1 teaspoon lemon juice
1 tablespoon chopped fresh parsley
6 slices pumpernickel
8 thin slices cucumber
8 radishes and 8 small parsley sprigs, to garnish

Put lobster into a bowl. Add celery and 2 tablespoons mayonnaise. Season with salt and cayenne pepper.

Mix butter with lemon juice and parsley. Using a 5 cm (2 in) fluted biscuit cutter, cut out 4 rounds from each slice of pumpernickel.

Butter 8 pumpernickel rounds on one side and remaining 16 on both sides. Cover 8 rounds buttered on one side with a slice of cucumber. Top with half the lobster mixture and place half the remaining rounds buttered on both sides on top. Repeat with rest of lobster mixture and bread rounds. Press together lightly.

Spread tops lightly with remaining mayonnaise. Cut radishes into dainty wedge-shaped slices and arrange like spokes of a wheel on top of each one. Garnish each sandwich with a small parsley sprig.

Makes 8

Variations: Use flaked white crabmeat or chopped cooked prawns instead of lobster, if preferred.

BRIE & APPLE SLICES

45 g (1½oz/9 teaspoons) butter, softened
15 g (½ oz/2 tablespoons) walnuts, chopped
4 square slices light rye bread, crusts removed
4 lengthwise slices Brie, about 0.5 cm (¼ in) thick
½ green eating apple
½ red eating apple
1 tablespoon lemon juice
watercress sprigs, to garnish

In a bowl, mix butter with walnuts until thoroughly combined. Spread mixture over the slices of bread.

Cut slices of cheese in half crosswise and arrange 2 pieces on each slice of bread.

Quarter apples and remove cores but do not peel. Slice apples thinly and brush the slices with the lemon juice.

Arrange overlapping alternate slices of green and red apple over cheese. Cut each slice of bread in half diagonally. Arrange on a serving plate, garnished with sprigs of watercress.

Makes 8.

SPICY PRAWN TEMPTERS

125 g (4 oz) peeled cooked prawns, thawed
if frozen and coarsely chopped

2 tablespoons thousand island dressing

2 teaspoons tomato purée (paste)

1 teaspoon creamed horseradish sauce

salt and pepper

45 g (1½ oz/9 teaspoons) butter,
softened

4 slices light rye bread, crusts removed

few watercress sprigs

4 small radicchio leaves

watercress sprigs and peeled prawns
(optional), to garnish

In a bowl, mix prawns with dressing, tomato purée and horseradish sauce, then season with salt and pepper.

Butter slices of bread. Cover 2 slices with watercress sprigs and top with prawn mixture. Cover with radicchio leaves. Place remaining slices of bread in position, buttered side down.

Press sandwiches together firmly and cut diagonally into quarters. Arrange on a serving plate, garnished with sprigs of watercress and prawns, if desired.

Makes 8.

Variations: Use thinly sliced *daktyla* (Greek sesame seed bread), if preferred, but do not cut off crusts.

Omit radicchio and use crisp green lettuce leaves instead.

PIQUANT SALMON TREATS

185 g (6 oz) fresh salmon steak

1 teaspoon lemon juice

salt and pepper

3 tablespoons mayonnaise

1-2 teaspoons capers, drained

3 cocktail gherkins, chopped

1 spring onion, chopped

2 lengthwise slices from uncut white
sandwich loaf, about 0.5 cm (¼ in) thick,
crusts removed

45 g (1½ oz/9 teaspoons) butter,
softened

paprika for sprinkling

small parsley sprigs, to garnish

Preheat oven to 180C (350F/Gas 4). Put salmon on a buttered sheet of foil. Sprinkle with lemon juice and season with salt and pepper. Wrap foil to enclose salmon and put on a baking sheet. Cook for 25 minutes. Cool, then skin and bone.

Flake salmon into a bowl. Add mayonnaise. Dry capers well on absorbent kitchen paper; finely chop. Add capers, gherkins and spring onion to bowl. Season with salt and pepper and mix well.

Using a rolling pin, lightly roll slices of bread to flatten slightly. Butter 1 slice on one side and remaining slice on both sides. Using a 5 cm (2 in) fluted round biscuit cutter, cut out 8 rounds from slice buttered on one side. Cover these rounds with salmon mixture, reserving a little.

Using same cutter, cut out 8 rounds from remaining slice of bread, then, using a small 2 cm (¾ in) fluted round cutter, cut out centre from each round and discard. Sprinkle circles with paprika and place over salmon. Press lightly. Spoon remaining salmon into centres. Garnish with parsley.

Makes 8.

CHICKEN RELISH SWIRLS

90 g (3 oz) cold cooked chicken, skinned
2 teaspoons mango chutney, chopped
2 teaspoons mayonnaise
3 tablespoons finely chopped green
pepper (capsicum)
2 spring onions, finely chopped
2 cocktail gherkins, finely chopped
salt and pepper
3 medium-thick slices white bread, crusts
removed
60 g (2 oz/¼ cup) butter, softened
about 21 stuffed green olives
coriander sprigs, to garnish

Purée chicken in a food processor or
mince finely. In a bowl, mix
chicken and chutney with mayonnaise, green pepper (capsicum),
onions and gherkins. Season with
salt and pepper.

Using a rolling pin, roll each

slice of bread firmly to flatten.
Spread with butter, then spread
with chicken mixture.

Arrange a row of stuffed olives
along one shorter edge of each slice.
Roll up each slice of bread like a
Swiss roll. Wrap each roll tightly in
plastic film and chill for at least
2 hours.

Cut each roll at a slight diagonal
angle into 7 slices. Arrange slices
on a serving plate, garnished with
sprigs of coriander.

Makes 21.

Variations: Use cocktail gherkins
to replace stuffed olives.

Use cold cooked turkey instead
of chicken, or use a mixture of
chicken and ham.

DEVILLED CRAB TREATS

125 g (4 oz) white crabmeat, thawed if
frozen and well drained if canned
2 tablespoons mayonnaise
few drops lemon juice
few drops Tabasco sauce
¼ teaspoon dry mustard
salt and pepper
45 g (1½ oz/9 teaspoons) butter,
softened
4 thin slices brown or white bread from a
small loaf, crusts removed
1-2 crisp lettuce leaves, finely shredded
1 teaspoon paprika
lemon twist and watercress sprigs,
to garnish

Flake crabmeat into a bowl. Add all
but 1 teaspoon mayonnaise, lemon
juice, Tabasco sauce and mustard.
Season with salt and pepper, then
mix together lightly.

Butter slices of bread. Spread 2
slices with crab mixture and top
with shredded lettuce. Cover with

remaining slices of buttered bread.
Press together firmly and cut
diagonally into quarters.

Hold each sandwich by the long
straight edge and very lightly spread
reserved mayonnaise onto one
alternate edge of each sandwich.
Dip these coated edges into
paprika.

Arrange sandwiches on a serving
plate, standing them in rows of 4
with pointed ends upwards. Garnish with a lemon twist and
sprigs of watercress.

Makes 8.

Variations: Use peeled and thinly
sliced cucumber instead of finely
shredded lettuce.

Coat edges in finely chopped
chives instead of paprika, or for a
colourful combination, coat half in
paprika and remainder in chives.

SMOKED SALMON BAGELS

2 bagels
185 g (6 oz) full fat soft cheese
2 teaspoons lemon juice
2 tablespoons thick sour cream
3 spring onions, chopped
a little cayenne pepper
60-90 g (2-3 oz) thinly sliced smoked
salmon
spring onion flowers and lemon twists, to
garnish

Preheat oven to 180C (350F/ Gas 4). Wrap bagels in foil and heat in oven for 15 minutes.

Meanwhile, in a bowl, mix together cheese, lemon juice, sour cream and spring onions and season with cayenne pepper. Form smoked salmon into rolls and cut into thin slices.

Cut warmed bagels in half. Spread the bases with half of the cheese mixture. Arrange smoked salmon slices over bases, cover with remaining cheese mixture and sandwich bagels together with top halves. Garnish with spring onion flowers and lemon twists.

Makes 2.

PORK & CELERY CRUNCH

1 tablespoon mayonnaise
1 teaspoon French mustard
1 stick celery, chopped
1-2 teaspoons apple sauce (optional)
salt and pepper
30 g (1 oz/6 teaspoons) butter, softened
2 large chunky slices granary bread
1 chunky slice iceberg lettuce
2-3 slices cooked roast pork
a few red onion rings
small leafy sticks celery and red onion
rings, to garnish

In a bowl, mix mayonnaise with mustard, celery and apple sauce, if desired. Season with salt and pepper.

Butter slices of bread. Arrange lettuce slice on 1 slice of bread. Add slices of pork, folded over to fit neatly, and spoon celery mixture over pork. Cover with onion rings.

Place remaining slice of bread on top. Press together lightly and cut diagonally into quarters. Garnish with small leafy sticks celery and red onion rings.

Makes 4.

Variations: Omit pork and apple sauce and replace with cold roast beef or corned beef and horseradish sauce, if preferred.

SCOTCH EGG ROLLS

250 g (8 oz) pork sausagemeat
1 small onion, finely chopped
salt and pepper
2 hard-boiled eggs, shelled
1 tablespoon plain flour
1 egg, beaten
3 tablespoons dry breadcrumbs
vegetable oil for deep frying
4 cottage loaf rolls
90 g (3 oz/⅓ cup) butter, softened
curly endive leaves
2 large tomatoes, thinly sliced
2 tablespoons piccalilli
TO GARNISH:
curly endive sprigs
crisp bacon rolls
radish flowers

Put sausagemeat and onion in a bowl. Season with salt and pepper and mix well. Divide in half. Roll hard-boiled eggs in flour and, with floured hands, wrap eggs in sausagemeat mixture to enclose completely. Smooth over joins, then dip in beaten egg and roll in breadcrumbs, pressing on firmly.

Half fill a deep-fat fryer or pan with oil and heat to 190C (375F) or until a cube of day-old bread browns in 40 seconds. Fry eggs 6 minutes until golden. Drain and cool.

Cut off top portions of rolls and spread with butter. Cut a thin slice from base of rolls and spread each cut side with butter. Scoop out soft bread from centre sections of rolls, large enough to take a halved Scotch egg. Spread with butter.

Cover base slices with endive and tomato. Place centre sections on top. Cut eggs in half, press into holes in rolls and top with piccalilli. Add lids at an angle and secure with cocktail sticks threaded with endive, bacon rolls and radishes.

Makes 4.

TUNA-AVOCADO SANDWICHES

99 g (3½ oz) can tuna in oil, drained
2 spring onions, chopped
2 tablespoons tartare sauce
salt and pepper
1 ripe avocado
1 tablespoon lemon juice
60 g (2 oz/¼ cup) butter, softened
4 slices light rye bread
TO GARNISH:
small wedges of lemon
avocado slices
parsley sprigs

Flake tuna into a bowl. Add spring onions and 1 tablespoon tartare sauce. Season to taste with salt and pepper and mix well together.

Halve avocado and remove stone. Peel avocado and cut into slices, then dip in lemon juice.

Butter slices of bread. Cover 2 slices with tuna mixture and top with avocado slices. Spread with remaining tartare sauce and season with salt and pepper.

Cover with remaining bread slices and press together firmly. Cut diagonally into halves. Garnish with small wedges of lemon, avocado slices and sprigs of parsley.

Makes 4.

PÂTÉ & SALAD CROISSANTS

2 croissants
30 g (1 oz/6 teaspoons) butter, softened
45 g (1½ oz) Boursin cheese
6 small hearty Little Gem lettuce leaves
6 large slices beefsteak tomato, halved
125 g (4 oz) firm pâté, sliced
salt and pepper
TO GARNISH:
2 crisp bacon rolls
2 black olives
2 small lettuce leaves

Cut croissants two-thirds way through centres, cutting from rounded sides through to pointed sides but do not cut right through. Open out slightly and spread both sides lightly with butter.

Spread one side with Boursin cheese and add lettuce leaves, set at an angle. Add 3 tomato slices to each croissant and arrange slices of pâté along one side. Place remaining halves of tomato slices along other side of pâté and season with salt and pepper.

To garnish, thread bacon rolls, olives and small lettuce leaves onto 2 cocktail sticks and secure one into each croissant.

Makes 2.

Variations: Top filled croissants with a little mayonnaise or pickle of your choice, if wished.

STILTON-PEAR TOPPER

7 g (¼ oz/1½ teaspoons) unsalted butter, softened
1 slice crusty granary bread
few curly endive sprigs
½ ripe pear, cored and sliced
1 teaspoon lemon juice
2 slices Stilton cheese
1 walnut half
lemon twist and 2 small watercress sprigs, to garnish

Spread butter over the slice of bread. Place curly endive sprigs over buttered bread and press down.

Brush slices of pear with lemon juice. Place slices of cheese on bread and arrange slices of pear in an overlapping fan-shape to one side of cheese.

Add the walnut half and garnish with a lemon twist and small sprigs of watercress.

Makes 1.

Variations: Use Danish blue, Cambozola, Dolcelatte or Roquefort cheese instead of Stilton. Replace pear slices with slices of star fruit.

POTTED PRAWN TREAT

45 g (1½ oz/9 teaspoons) unsalted butter, plus 7 g (¼ oz/1½ teaspoons) for spreading

60 g (2 oz) peeled cooked prawns, coarsely chopped, see Note

½ small clove garlic, crushed

pinch ground cumin

pinch ground mace

2 pinches cayenne pepper

1 teaspoon finely chopped fresh parsley

salt and white pepper

1 slice pumpernickel

3-4 small radicchio leaves

TO GARNISH:

several flat-leaf parsley sprigs

peeled or unpeeled cooked prawns

Melt 15g (½ oz/3 teaspoons) butter in a saucepan. Add prawns and garlic and cook gently for 1 minute. Remove from heat and stir in cumin, mace, cayenne pepper and parsley. Season with salt and white pepper and mix well. Spoon into a 125 ml (4 fl oz/½ cup) capacity ramekin and level surface.

Melt 30 g (1 oz/6 teaspoons) remaining butter in a pan, then cool slightly. Pour over prawn mixture. Cool, then chill for 2 hours or until set.

Spread remaining butter over pumpernickel and top with radicchio leaves. Run a knife around edges of ramekin to loosen prawn mould and turn out. Place mould in centre of sandwich and surround with sprigs of flat-leaf parsley. Garnish with prawns.

Makes 1.

Note: If using thawed frozen prawns, the thawed weight should be 60 g (2 oz). Squeeze thawed prawns in absorbent paper to remove excess moisture.

SPICED EGG SLICE

1 hard-boiled egg, shelled and chopped

1 tablespoon mayonnaise

30 g (1 oz/¼ cup) Cheddar cheese, finely diced

1 spring onion, chopped

½-¾ teaspoon concentrated curry paste

salt and pepper

7 g (¼ oz/1½ teaspoons) butter, softened

1 slice pumpernickel

16 cucumber slices

3 small radish flowers and mint sprigs, to garnish

In a bowl, mix together hard-boiled egg, mayonnaise, cheese, spring onion and curry paste. Season with salt and pepper.

Spread butter over slice of pumpernickel. Arrange overlapping slices of cucumber all the way round edges, allowing slices to slightly overlap edges of bread.

Spoon curried egg mixture into centre and level slightly to neaten and to cover inner edges of cucumber slices. Garnish with radish flowers and sprigs of mint.

Makes 1.

Variations: Use thick sour cream instead of mayonnaise and 1 tablespoon chopped fresh chives instead of spring onion.

BEEF & CHICORY CRUNCH

7 g (¼ oz/1½ teaspoons) unsalted butter,
softened

1 slice pumpernickel

4-5 chicory leaves

1 teaspoon mayonnaise

1 teaspoon creamed horseradish sauce

2 slices rare roast beef

1 tablespoon pickled red cabbage, drained

dill sprigs and cucumber twists, to garnish

Spread butter over the slice of
pumpernickel. Arrange chicory
leaves at an angle over bread.

Mix mayonnaise with horseradish sauce and spread over slices
of beef. Fold beef slices and arrange
over chicory. Spoon red cabbage
onto sandwich. Garnish with sprigs
of dill and cucumber twists.

Makes 1.

Variations: Use slices of cooked
ham or tongue instead of rare beef.
Finely shredded radicchio leaves,
tossed in French dressing, make a
tasty change from pickled red
cabbage.

CHILLIED SALAMI HERO

½ small French stick, or large, long
granary roll

45 g (1½ oz/9 teaspoons) butter, softened

1 small clove garlic, crushed

1-2 tablespoons chopped canned green
chilli

½ ripe avocado

1 teaspoon lemon juice

4 slices salami, rinded

1 slice processed Cheddar cheese, cut
diagonally into quarters

cherry tomatoes and pickled whole
chillies, to garnish (optional)

Cut French stick or roll lengthwise
two-thirds way up from base, but do
not cut right through. Open out roll
sufficiently to take the filling. In a
bowl, mix butter with garlic and
spread over roll. Sprinkle base with
chopped chilli.

Peel avocado and cut into slices,
then dip in lemon juice. Arrange
along base of roll to create a fan-
shape. Fold slices of salami into
quarters and arrange over avocado.
Arrange cheese slices on top of
salami.

Garnish with 2 or 3 cocktail
sticks, threaded with cherry
tomatoes and pickled chillies, if
desired.

Makes 1.

CHEESE & HAM ROLL-UPS

1 short sesame-seeded French stick	
60 g (2 oz/¼ cup) butter, softened	
1 teaspoon prepared mustard	
2-3 tablespoons mayonnaise	
3 square slices cooked ham	
250 g (8 oz) ricotta cheese	
1 carton cress	
salt and pepper	
18 slices cucumber	
3 small tomatoes, thinly sliced	
6 watercress sprigs, to garnish	

Cut out 6 'V' shaped pieces at regular intervals along French stick, each deep and wide enough to hold a stuffed ham roll plus cucumber and tomato slices along each edge.

Mix butter with mustard and spread over 'V' shapes, then spread with mayonnaise.

Spread ham slices with ricotta cheese. Arrange cress, green parts facing outwards, along 2 opposite edges and season with salt and pepper. Roll up ham to show green cress at either end. Carefully cut each ham roll in half to make 6 small rolls.

Place overlapping cucumber and tomato slices along the edges of each 'V' shaped cut.

Place a ham roll in each 'V' shape and garnish each one with a watercress sprig. Serve cut into chunky slices.

Makes 6.

SAUCY SEAFOOD LOAF

1 short French stick	
90 g (3 oz/⅓ cup) butter	
1 onion, finely chopped	
60 g (2 oz/½ cup) plain flour	
315 ml (10 fl oz/1¼ cups) milk	
125 ml (4 fl oz/½ cup) single (light) cream	
2 tablespoons dry white wine	
185 g (6 oz) peeled cooked prawns, thawed if frozen	
185 g (6 oz) salmon steak, cooked, see page 16	
2 tablespoons chopped fresh parsley	
salt and pepper	
30 g (1 oz/¼ cup) Emmental or Cheddar cheese, grated	
lemon slices and unpeeled cooked prawns and parsley, to garnish	

Preheat oven to 190C (375F/Gas 5). Cut loaf centrally along top but do not cut right through. Open out slightly and pull out soft bread from both sides, leaving shell intact. Make about 45 g (1½ oz) of the bread into crumbs.

Melt 60 g (2 oz/¼ cup) butter in a saucepan, add onion and fry for 3 minutes. Stir in flour and cook for 1 minute, then gradually stir in milk and cream and bring to the boil, stirring. Simmer for 2 minutes. Add wine, prawns, salmon and parsley. Season with salt and pepper.

Spoon mixture into French stick and place on a sheet of foil on a baking sheet. Melt remaining butter in a pan, remove from heat and add breadcrumbs. Mix well, then sprinkle over filling in French stick. Sprinkle with cheese. Wrap foil around sides of loaf, leaving top exposed.

Cook for 20-25 minutes until topping is golden. Garnish with lemon slices, prawns and parsley. Cut into 4 and serve hot.

Serves 4.

CHICKEN MARYLAND ROLLS

4 crusty poppy seed knot-shaped rolls
90 g (3 oz/⅓ cup) butter, softened
2 skinned chicken breasts (fillets)
salt and pepper
60 g (2 oz/½ cup) plain flour
1 egg
1 tablespoon milk
2 spring onions, chopped
2 potatoes, grated
4 tablespoons sweetcorn kernels, drained if canned and thawed if frozen
vegetable oil for frying
2 small bananas
a little shredded lettuce
a little tomato relish
2 tomatoes, thinly sliced
watercress sprigs, to garnish

Cut the rolls in half and spread with 60 g (2 oz/¼ cup) butter. Cut each chicken breast into 4 thin slices by cutting at an angle through each. Season with salt and pepper.

In a bowl, mix flour with egg and milk. Add onions, potatoes and corn. Season and mix well. Heat oil in a large frying pan. Divide corn mixture into 4 and press out in pan into rounds the same size as rolls. Fry for 6 minutes, turning once, until golden. Drain and keep warm.

Pour off oil from pan. Add remaining butter to pan and fry chicken for 2-3 minutes on each side. Drain and keep warm. Cut bananas in half crosswise and then in half lengthwise. Add to pan and fry for 30-45 seconds.

Arrange a little lettuce on rolls; spread with relish and top each with a corn fritter. Add slices of tomato, 2 slices of chicken and 2 slices of banana to each one.

Secure lids in position with cocktail sticks and garnish with sprigs of watercress.

Makes 4.

STUFFED FRENCH STICK

125 g (4 oz) sliced garlic sausage, chopped
60 g (2 oz/½ cup) salted cashews, chopped
4 spring onions, chopped
1 small green pepper (capsicum), seeded and chopped
2 sticks celery, chopped
250 g (8 oz) cream cheese with chives
4 teaspoons tomato purée (paste)
1 clove garlic, crushed
salt and pepper
1 short granary French stick
spring onion flowers and small tomato water lilies, to garnish

In a bowl, mix together garlic sausage, nuts, onions, green pepper (capsicum), celery, cream cheese, tomato purée (paste) and garlic. Season with salt and pepper and mix well.

Cut French stick in half crosswise. Cut crusty ends off French stick pieces and, using a sharp, pointed knife, cut away soft bread from inside each piece, leaving crust intact.

Using a teaspoon, fill centres of French stick with cream cheese mixture, pushing in well from both ends to prevent any gaps in filling.

Wrap in foil and chill for 2 hours. Cut each piece into 10 slices and garnish with spring onion flowers and tomato water lilies.

Makes 20.

Variations: Use any flavour cream cheese of your choice, or use fromage frais, if preferred.

DESSERTS

GRAND MARNIER KEBABS

3 firm apricots
3 firm fresh figs
two 2.5 cm (1 in) thick trimmed pineapple slices
2 satsumas
2 firm bananas
2 eating apples
1 tablespoon lemon juice
90 g (3 oz/⅓ cup) unsalted butter
90 g (3 oz/½ cup) icing sugar
1 tablespoon Grand Marnier
1 tablespoon fresh orange juice
1 tablespoon finely grated orange peel

Halve apricots and remove stones. Remove stalks and quarter figs lengthwise.

Remove any woody core and cut pineapple slices into chunks. Peel satsumas and quarter but do not remove membranes. Peel bananas and cut into 2.5 cm (1 in) thick slices. Peel apples, cut into quarters, remove cores and halve each apple piece crosswise. Sprinkle apples and bananas with lemon juice to prevent discoloration.

Thread fruit onto 6-8 skewers, making sure that each has a mixture of fruit and starting and finishing with apple and pineapple. Melt butter, stir in icing sugar, then add Grand Marnier, orange juice and peel. Brush kebabs with sauce and barbecue over medium coals for 5-6 minutes, frequently basting with sauce. Serve any remaining sauce with kebabs. Serve hot.

Serves 6-8.

PRALINE BANANAS

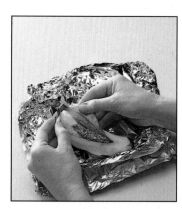

15 g (½ oz) unskinned almonds
15 g (½ oz) unskinned hazelnuts
60 g (2 oz/¼ cup) granulated sugar
6 under-ripe bananas
whipped cream, to serve

Put almonds, hazelnuts and sugar in a small, heavy-based frying pan. Heat gently, stirring constantly until sugar dissolves. Raise heat and cook to a deep brown syrup. Immediately, pour onto a sheet of non-stick paper placed on a metal baking sheet on a wooden board. The toffee-like mixture will be very hot. Leave until cold and brittle; crush finely.

Lay unpeeled bananas flat and make a slit through the skin along top surface. Slightly open out the skin and fill each slit with about 3 teaspoons of praline. Re-shape the bananas and wrap individually and tightly in double thickness foil, sealing along the top.

Barbecue directly on medium coals for 8-10 minutes, turning packets over halfway through cooking time. To serve, unfold foil wrapping and slightly open banana skins. Serve with whipped cream.

Serves 6.

PEACHES & BUTTERSCOTCH

6 peaches, halved and stoned
angelica, to decorate, if desired

BUTTERSCOTCH SAUCE: 90 g (3 oz/½ cup) light soft
 brown sugar
155 ml (5 fl oz/⅔ cup) maple syrup
45 g (1½ oz/3 tablespoons) butter
pinch of salt
155 ml (5 fl oz/⅔ cup) single (light) cream
few drops vanilla essence

FILLING: 60 g (2 oz/½ cup) ground almonds
2 tablespoons finely chopped angelica

Wash, dry and halve peaches; remove stones.

To make sauce, combine sugar, maple syrup,
butter and salt in a heavy-based saucepan.
Bring to boil, stir once, then boil for 3
minutes to form a thick syrup. Stir in cream,
bring back to boil and immediately remove
from heat. Stir in vanilla essence to taste.
Pour into a jug and keep warm.

Put peach halves, cut-sides down, on
individual squares of double thickness foil.
Curl up sides of foil but do not seal. Barbecue
on rack over hot coals for 5 minutes. Turn
peaches over on the foil; spoon almonds and
angelica into cavities and pour over a
tablespoon of butterscotch sauce. Draw up
edges of foil and twist above peaches to seal.
Barbecue for 10 minutes until tender.
Decorate with angelica, if desired, and serve
hot with remaining sauce.

Serves 6-12.

VODKA-SOUSED PINEAPPLE

4 large, fresh 2 cm (¾ in) thick pineapple slices
3 tablespoons vodka
90 g (3 oz/⅓ cup) unsalted butter
60 ml (2 fl oz/¼ cup) double (thick) cream
1 teaspoon ground cardamom
2 tablespoons icing sugar
12 bottled morello cherries
icing sugar for dusting

Peel pineapple and remove central core. Pour
vodka into a shallow dish, add pineapple
slices, then turn slices over once. Cover dish
and leave to marinate for 20 minutes.

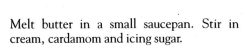

Melt butter in a small saucepan. Stir in
cream, cardamom and icing sugar.

Dip pineapple slices into melted butter
mixture and barbecue on rack over hot coals
for 5 minutes on each side until golden
brown. Serve on warm plates, with pineapple
centres filled with morello cherries. Dust
lightly with icing sugar.

Serves 4.

RUM & RAISIN SHARON FRUIT

6 firm sharon fruit
30 g (1 oz/2 tablespoons) mixed dried fruit
1 glacé cherry
3 unskinned almonds
2 teaspoons dark soft brown sugar
1 teaspoon dark rum
pinch of ground cinnamon
½ teaspoon lemon juice
6 small strawberries

Remove stalks from sharon fruit and, using a teaspoon, scoop out pulp, leaving fleshy wall intact. Put pulp in a bowl.

Using a sharp, lightly-floured knife, very finely chop dried fruit, cherry and almonds. Mix into fruit pulp, adding sugar, rum, cinnamon and lemon juice. Carefully pack filling into sharon shells and wrap separately in lightly oiled, double thickness foil.

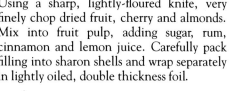

Place foil parcels in medium coals and cook for 25-30 minutes until fruit is soft. To serve, unwrap and top each one with a strawberry.

Serves 6.

HOT TROPICANAS

3 pink grapefruit
8 lychees
2 kumquats, rinsed and dried
1 guava
1 pawpaw
1 small mango
4 tablespoons golden syrup
30 g (1 oz/6 teaspoons) butter
2 tablespoons desiccated coconut, toasted

Halve grapefruit, separate and remove segments and drain. Scrape out grapefruit shells, discarding membranes.

Peel and stone lychees. Slice kumquats. Halve guava and pawpaw. Scoop out seeds, then peel and dice flesh. Peel mango, pare flesh away from stone and cut into strips. Combine all fruits in a bowl. Melt syrup, pour over fruits and mix gently.

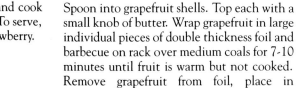

Spoon into grapefruit shells. Top each with a small knob of butter. Wrap grapefruit in large individual pieces of double thickness foil and barbecue on rack over medium coals for 7-10 minutes until fruit is warm but not cooked. Remove grapefruit from foil, place in individual dishes and top with toasted coconut.

Serves 6.

Note: Decorate the grapefruit with sprigs of mint, if desired.

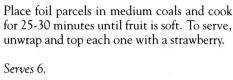

PEAR & PEACH APPLES

2 dried pear halves
2 dried peach halves
1 tablespoon sultanas
good pinch of ground cloves
pinch of mixed spice
60 g (2 oz/⅓ cup) light soft brown sugar
30 g (1 oz/6 teaspoons) butter
4 cooking apples
whipped cream, to serve

Put pear and peach halves in a saucepan. Add sufficient water to just cover fruits, then bring to boil and cook for 5 minutes. Drain thoroughly, then chop. Mix with sultanas, spices, sugar and butter.

Wash and core apples. Put on individual squares of double thickness foil. Stuff cavities with fruit filling, packing it in firmly. Draw up edges of foil and twist firmly to secure over apples.

Barbecue on rack over medium coals for 45-50 minutes. Using twisted foil as an aid, turn apples on their sides from time to time. Alternatively, cook directly in coals without turning for 20-30 minutes. To serve, snip off foil stalks and fold foil back to expose apples. Serve with whipped cream.

Serves 4.

KIWIS & STEM GINGER

6 pieces preserved stem ginger in syrup
6 firm kiwi fruit, unpeeled
5-6 tablespoons preserved stem ginger syrup
155 ml (5 fl oz/⅔ cup) whipping cream
3 teaspoons icing sugar
1 tablespoon chopped shelled pistachio nuts

Cut pieces of stem ginger in half lengthwise. Rinse and dry kiwi fruit and halve lengthwise. Remove firm cores, chop and reserve. Spoon a little ginger syrup over kiwi flesh and pierce with a skewer to help absorption. Stiffly whip cream with sugar and refrigerate until required.

Place the ginger in cavities in kiwi fruit. Place filled kiwi halves, skin-sides down, onto squares of foil and pour a little more ginger syrup over ginger. Wrap up securely.

Barbecue over medium hot coals for 10-15 minutes, turning packets over towards end of cooking time. Serve in open packets, cut-sides of fruit uppermost. Sprinkle with nuts and reserved chopped cores. Serve with the sweetened whipped cream.

Serves 6.

Note: This dish can also be served as a starter – in which case omit the cream and sugar.

BRANDIED FRUIT CRÊPES

185 g (6 oz/¾ cup) caster sugar
4 strips pared lemon peel
125 g (4 oz) kumquats
3 nectarines, sliced
butter for frying
60 ml (2 fl oz/¼ cup) apricot brandy
mint leaves or tiny flowers, to decorate
BATTER:
125 g (4 oz/1 cup) plain flour
155 ml (5 fl oz/⅔ cup) milk
1 egg

Gently heat sugar, lemon peel and 315 ml (10 fl oz/1¼ cups) water in a saucepan until sugar has dissolved. Add kumquats and bring to the boil, then cover and cook gently for 5 minutes, until tender.

Pour kumquats into a bowl, add nectarines and set aside until cold.

Meanwhile, to make batter, place flour in a bowl and mix milk and egg together with 155 ml (5 fl oz/⅔ cup) water in a jug, whisking until well blended. Make a well in centre of flour and add half milk mixture, beating well with a wooden spoon. Add remaining milk, beating well.

Melt enough butter to lightly grease a small frying pan. Pour in enough batter to just thinly coat base of pan and swirl pan to spread the batter. Cook for about 1 minute on each side.

Place crêpe on a plate covered with kitchen paper; repeat to make 10-12 crêpes. Cover and keep warm.

Strain syrup from fruit into a saucepan, boil rapidly for 3-4 minutes, until thick. Cool slightly, stir in brandy and pour over fruit.

Fold crêpes into 4 making a triangle and serve with kumquats, nectarines and syrup. Decorate with mint leaves or tiny flowers.

Serves 4.

FIG & PORT ICE CREAM

125 g (4 oz/½ cup) caster sugar
155 ml (5 fl oz/⅔ cup) ruby port
4 cm (1½ in) cinnamon stick
6 fresh figs
4 teaspoons freshly squeezed lime juice
315 ml (10 fl oz/1¼ cups) double (thick) cream
fresh fig slices and mint leaves, to decorate

Place sugar and port in a saucepan and heat gently, stirring occasionally, until sugar has melted. Bring to the boil, then add cinnamon stick and figs, cover and cook very gently for 5 minutes. Leave the figs in the marinade, still covered, until they are completely cold.

Transfer figs and liquor to a food processor fitted with a metal blade and process until smooth.

Pour mixture into a sieve over a bowl and rub through using a wooden spoon. Stir in lime juice.

Whip cream until thick, then fold into fig purée until evenly blended. Pour mixture into a plastic container, cover and freeze for 1-2 hours, until almost frozen.

Return mixture to food processor and process until thick and smooth. Return to plastic container and freeze until firm. Scoop ice cream to serve, then decorate.

Serves 4.

FRUIT KEBABS

4 teaspoons dark rum or sherry

60 g (2 oz/¼ cup) caster sugar

½ fresh pineapple, flesh cut into bite-size pieces with juice reserved

2 oranges, peeled with all white pith removed and segmented with juice reserved

2 nectarines, sliced

24 cherries, stoned

2 bananas, sliced

2 teaspoons lemon juice

2 teaspoons ground cinnamon

155 ml (5 fl oz/⅔ cup) double (thick) cream

Mix rum and half the sugar together in a large bowl. Add pineapple and oranges with any reserved juices and nectarines and cherries.

Toss banana slices in lemon juice to prevent discoloration, then add to bowl; turn fruit in marinade to coat evenly. Cover with plastic wrap and leave for 15 minutes.

Mix together remaining sugar and cinnamon on a flat plate. Fill 6 thin wooden skewers with a mixture of fruit.

Roll each kebab in the sugar and cinnamon mixture to coat evenly. Whip cream until thick, add remaining marinade juices and fold in carefully until well blended. Place in a serving bowl.

Prepare barbecue or preheat grill. Cook kebabs for 2-3 minutes, turning once, until hot and tinged with brown. Serve with the cream.

Serves 6.

MIXED FRUIT TARTS

2 figs, sliced

8 teaspoons blackcurrants

90 g (3 oz) white grapes

1 peach, peeled and sliced

125 g (4 oz/½ cup) cream cheese

155 g (5 oz/⅔ cup) natural yogurt

1 teaspoon arrowroot

SWEET PASTRY:

125 g (4 oz/1 cup) plain flour

90 g (3 oz/⅓ cup) unsalted butter, chilled and diced

30 g (1 oz/5 teaspoons) caster sugar

1 egg yolk

MARINADE:

8 teaspoons grenadine syrup

8 teaspoons white wine or cider

6 teaspoons chopped fresh apple mint

To make pastry, put flour in a mixing bowl and rub in butter until mixture resembles breadcrumbs. Stir in sugar and egg yolk and mix to a soft dough. Wrap in plastic wrap and chill for 30 minutes.

To make marinade, mix grenadine, wine or cider and mint together in a bowl. Add fig slices, blackcurrants, grapes and peach. Turn to coat with marinade. Cover with plastic wrap and chill.

Preheat oven to 190C (375F/Gas 5). Roll out pastry thinly and line 8 individual brioche moulds or tart tins. Prick pastry with a fork and chill until firm. Bake for 8-10 minutes, until pastry is pale in colour. Cool in tin for 5 minutes, then turn out onto a wire rack.

Mix cream cheese and yogurt together. Strain marinade from fruit into a small saucepan, blend in arrowroot and bring to the boil, stirring. Cook for 30 seconds; cool.

Fill each tartlet with cream cheese mixture and fruit and glaze with marinade.

Makes 8.

JEWELLED FRUIT JELLY

470 ml (15 fl oz/2 cups) red grape juice
470 ml (15 fl oz/2 cups) white grape juice
6 teaspoons gelatine
1 star fruit, sliced
125 g (4 oz) white seedless grapes
125 g (4 oz) cherries, stoned
125 g (4 oz) strawberries, halved and sliced
strawberry leaves and flowers, to decorate
MARINADE:
4 teaspoons orange flower water or Cointreau
4 teaspoons rosewater or kirsch
8 teaspoons icing sugar

Pour red and white grape juices into separate bowls. Sprinkle gelatine over 90 ml (3 fl oz/⅓ cup) water in a bowl and stir. Dissolve over a pan of hot water until clear, then stir half into each bowl of juice.

To make marinade, pour flower water or Cointreau, and rosewater or kirsch onto separate plates; sift half the icing sugar on to each. Add star fruit and grapes to flower water or Cointreau, and cherries and strawberries to rosewater or kirsch. Cover and leave 30 minutes.

Using a 1.5 litre (2½ pint/6 cup) fluted mould or 8 individual moulds, pour 1 cm (½ in) white juice into mould. Cool until just setting.

Arrange one-third star fruit and grapes over jelly, spoon over white juice to cover; leave until set.

Arrange one-third cherries and strawberries over white jelly layer, then cover with red juice and leave to set. Repeat layering until all fruit and juices have been used. Leave for 1 hour until jelly has set.

Dip mould into hand-hot water for 1-2 seconds, then invert on to a serving plate. Decorate with extra fruit or leaves and flowers.

Serves 8.

FRUIT CHEESE DESSERT

60 ml (2 fl oz/¼ cup) Marsala
¼ teaspoon ground mace
185 g (6 oz/1 cup) mixed glacé fruit, chopped
375 g (12 oz/1½ cups) ricotta or cream cheese
4 teaspoons caster sugar
2 eggs, separated
2 teaspoons grated lemon peel
155 ml (5 fl oz/⅔ cup) whipping cream
fresh or glacé fruit and mint leaves, to decorate

Mix Marsala, mace and glacé fruit together in a bowl, stirring until well blended. Cover with plastic wrap and leave for several hours.

Put ricotta or cream cheese into a bowl, add sugar, egg yolks and lemon peel, beating with a wooden spoon until smooth. Add marinated fruit and stir until well mixed with the cheese.

Whisk egg whites; whip cream until it peaks softly. Fold alternately into cheese mixture.

Spoon into 6 small dishes and chill for 1 hour before serving. Decorate top of each dessert with fresh or glacé fruit and a mint leaf.

Serves 6.

ROSE PETAL PAVLOVAS

3 egg whites
220 g (7 oz/1 cup) caster sugar
1 teaspoon rosewater
1 teaspoon raspberry vinegar
1 teaspoon cornflour
rose pink food colouring
90 g (3 oz) raspberries
90 g (3 oz) strawberries, hulled and sliced
125 g (4 oz) redcurrants or cherries, stoned
315 ml (10 fl oz/1¼ cups) double (thick) cream
125 g (4 oz/½ cup) strained Greek yogurt
rose petals for decoration
MARINADE:
4 teaspoons rosewater
4 teaspoons rosé wine
8 teaspoons icing sugar, sifted
petals from 2 scented roses

Preheat oven to 120C (250F/Gas ½). Line 2 baking sheets with baking parchment.

Whisk egg whites until stiff, then add sugar a little at a time, whisking well after each addition, until thick. Mix rosewater, vinegar, cornflour and a drop of pink food colouring together. Add to meringue and whisk until thick and glossy.

Place 12 dessertspoonfuls of meringue, spaced apart, onto baking sheet. Bake for 45 minutes. Turn off oven and leave until cold.

To make marinade, mix rosewater, rosé wine, icing sugar and rose petals together. Add fruit and turn carefully to coat evenly. Cover with plastic wrap and chill for 30 minutes.

Whip cream until thick, fold in yogurt and strain in marinade.

Arrange pavlovas on a serving plate, spoon cream onto each, top with fruit and decorate with petals.

Makes 12.

TIPSY FRUIT CLOUD

2 kiwi fruit, peeled and cubed
2 peaches, peeled, stoned and cubed
½ pineapple, peeled, cored and cubed
185 g (6 oz) strawberries, hulled
125 g (4 oz/½ cup) fromage frais
125 ml (4 fl oz/½ cup) double (thick) cream
mint leaves, to decorate
MARINADE
3 teaspoons dark rum
3 teaspoons kirsch
3 teaspoons peach brandy
60 g (2 oz/½ cup) icing sugar, sifted
2 teaspoons finely grated orange peel

To make marinade, mix rum, kirsch, brandy, icing sugar and orange peel together in a shallow dish.

Add all fruit to marinade and turn carefully to coat evenly. Cover with plastic wrap and chill for 1-2 hours to marinate.

Whip fromage frais and cream together until thick. Strain marinade from mixed fruit into a bowl. Reserve a few pieces of fruit for decoration and carefully fold remaining fruit into cream mixture.

Divide fruit between 6 glasses and decorate with fresh mint leaves and top with reserved fruit. Serve the marinade as a sauce.

Serves 6.

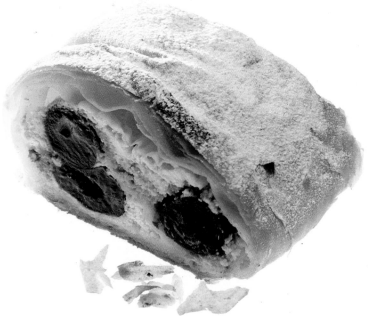

CHERRY CHEESE STRUDEL

185 g (6 oz) Ricotta cheese
125 g (4 oz) cottage cheese
60 ml (2 fl oz/¼ cup) thick sour cream
3 tablespoons ground almonds
220 g (7 oz/1 cup) butter
125 g (4 oz/2 cups) fresh breadcrumbs
8 sheets filo pastry
375 g (12 oz) can black cherries
90 g (3 oz/⅓ cup) dark soft brown sugar
TO SERVE:
icing sugar
single (light) cream

Preheat oven to 200C (400F/Gas 6). In a bowl, beat cheeses and sour cream. Stir in almonds. In a large frying pan, melt 90 g (3 oz/⅓ cup) of the butter and fry breadcrumbs until golden.

Spread a clean tea towel on a table and dust with flour. Melt remaining butter in a saucepan. Place sheet of pastry on tea towel and brush with melted butter. Cover with a second sheet of pastry and continue until pastry and most of the butter are used up. Spread cheese mixture over two-thirds of the pastry.

Drain cherries and arrange on cheese. Sprinkle fried breadcrumbs and brown sugar over cherries. Using the tea towel, roll up filling and pastry into a long sausage. Brush pastry with remaining melted butter. Bake in the oven for 40 minutes until golden. Dust with icing sugar and serve with cream.

Serves 8.

BLACKBERRY CHEESECAKE

125 g (4 oz/½ cup) butter
6 teaspoons light soft brown sugar
250 g (8 oz/2 cups) rolled oats
FILLING:
500 g (1 lb) Ricotta cheese
155 ml (5 fl oz/⅔ cup) thick sour cream
90 g (3 oz/⅓ cup) caster sugar
2 eggs
3 teaspoons plain flour
pinch of ground cloves
500 g (1 lb) cooking apples
90 g (3 oz) blackberries, thawed if frozen
TOPPING:
375 g (12 oz) blackberries, thawed if frozen
90 g (3 oz/¼ cup) redcurrant jelly
155 ml (5 fl oz/⅔ cup) whipping cream
10 sprigs of mint

Preheat oven to 180C (350F/Gas 4). Grease and line a 20 cm (8 in) round, loose-bottomed cake tin. In a saucepan, melt butter, then stir in brown sugar and oats. Mix well, then press into cake tin.

In a bowl, beat cheese, sour cream, sugar and eggs. Add flour and cloves and beat until smooth. Peel, core and chop apples. Stir into cheese with the 90 g (3 oz) blackberries. Spoon onto biscuit base and bake in the oven for 45 minutes. Leave to cool before removing from tin.

To make topping, arrange blackberries in centre of cheesecake. Melt redcurrant jelly in a small saucepan, then brush over blackberries. Whip cream and pipe a border of 10 rosettes around edge of cheesecake. Top each rosette with a mint sprig.

Serves 8–10.

RHUBARB & CUSTARD CAKE

60 g (2 oz/¼ cup) butter	
125 g (4 oz/1¼ cups) ginger biscuit crumbs	
FILLING:	
6 teaspoons cornflour	
250 ml (8 fl oz/1 cup) milk	
3 egg yolks	
few drops vanilla essence	
4 teaspoons powdered gelatine	
375 g (12 oz) medium fat soft cheese	
TOPPING:	
1 kg (2 lb) rhubarb	
90 g (3 oz/⅓ cup) caster sugar	
625 ml (20 fl oz/2½ cups) boiling water	

Grease a 22.5 cm (9 in) round, loose-bottomed cake tin. In a saucepan, melt butter, then stir in biscuit crumbs. Mix well, then press into base of cake tin.

In a heatproof bowl, mix cornflour with 3 tablespoons milk. Add egg yolks and vanilla essence. Stir well. In a saucepan, bring remaining milk to the boil. Pour into bowl and stir well, then pour back into saucepan and simmer to thicken.

Sprinkle gelatine over 2 tablespoons water in a small bowl and leave to soften for 2–3 minutes. Stir into custard and leave to cool.

Put cheese in a bowl. When custard has cooled and nearly set, blend a little at a time into cheese. Pour onto biscuit base and leave to set in the refrigerator for 2–3 hours.

Meanwhile, prepare topping. Cut rhubarb into 6 cm (2½ in) slices. Arrange in a heatproof dish, sprinkle over sugar and pour over boiling water. Cover and leave to cook in its own heat for 25–30 minutes.

When cheesecake has set, remove from tin. Remove rhubarb from liquid and drain on a wire rack. Arrange pieces in a fan shape around edge of cheesecake. Chill.

Serves 8.

CAROUSEL DE FROMAGE

500 g (1 lb) medium fat soft cheese	
315 ml (10 fl oz/1¼ cups) whipping cream	
90 g (3 oz/⅓ cup) caster sugar	
3 eggs	
few drops vanilla essence	
TO DECORATE:	
2 eating apples	
2 pears	
185 g (6 oz) strawberries	
185 g (6 oz) raspberries	
125 g (4 oz) black grapes	
2 oranges	
1 kiwi fruit	
155 ml (5 fl oz/⅔ cup) whipping cream	
10 sprigs of mint	

Preheat oven to 190C (375F/Gas 5). Grease a 22.5 cm (9 in) ring mould. In a bowl, beat cheese and cream until smooth. Add sugar, eggs and vanilla essence and blend evenly. Spoon into ring mould.

Stand ring mould in a roasting tin and add enough boiling water to come halfway up sides of ring mould. Cover with aluminium foil and bake in the oven for 50 minutes. To test ring, pierce with a skewer – if it comes away cleanly the ring is cooked. Leave to cool before turning out.

To decorate, cut the fruits into even-sized pieces. Arrange them in centre of ring. Whip cream and pipe 10 rosettes of cream around edge. Top each with a sprig of mint.

Serves 8–10.

BLACKCURRANT INDIVIDUALS

6 tablespoons blackcurrant preserve
250 g (8 oz) medium fat curd cheese
90 ml (3 fl oz/⅓ cup) thick sour cream
finely grated peel and juice of ½ a lemon
1 egg
9 teaspoons caster sugar
TO DECORATE:
6 sprigs of mint
TO SERVE:
155 ml (5 fl oz/⅔ cup) whipping cream

Preheat oven to 180C (350F/Gas 4). Spread 1 tablespoon blackcurrant preserve into bottom of 6 ramekin dishes. Place ramekins in a roasting tin and set aside.

In a bowl, beat cheese and sour cream. Add lemon peel and juice, egg and sugar, and beat until smooth. Spoon mixture into ramekin dishes, dividing it equally between them.

Pour enough boiling water into roasting tin to come halfway up sides of ramekin dishes. Bake in the oven for 35 minutes. Leave to cool completely.

To serve, run the blade of a small knife around edge of each ramekin dish and turn out onto a serving dish. Decorate each cheesecake with a spring of mint and serve with loosely whipped cream.

Serves 6.

MANGO CHEESECAKE

60 g (2 oz/¼ cup) butter
155 g (5 oz/1⅓ cups) digestive biscuit crumbs
FILLING:
250 g (8 oz) full fat soft cheese
155 ml (5 fl oz/⅔ cup) natural yogurt
155 ml (5 fl oz/⅔ cup) thick sour cream
2 eggs, separated
90 g (3 oz/⅓ cup) caster sugar
3 teaspoons powdered gelatine
250 g (8 oz) raspberries
TO DECORATE:
440 g (14 oz) can mango in syrup
250 g (8 oz) raspberries
155 ml (5 fl oz/⅔ cup) whipping cream
8-10 sprigs of mint

Grease and line a 22.5 cm (9 in) round, loose-bottomed cake tin. In a saucepan, melt butter, then stir in biscuit crumbs. Mix well, then press into cake tin.

To make filling, beat cheese and yogurt in a bowl. Add sour cream, egg yolks and 60 g (2 oz/¼ cup) sugar and beat until smooth.

Sprinkle gelatine over 2 tablespoons water in a small bowl and leave to soften for 2–3 minutes. Stand the bowl in a saucepan of hot water and stir until dissolved and quite hot. Stir into cheese mixture.

Whisk egg whites in a bowl with remaining sugar until firm. Fold into cheese mixture with the raspberries. Turn into cake tin and leave to set in the refrigerator for 2–3 hours.

To decorate, slice mango into thin strips and arrange in a fan shape on the top of the cheesecake. Arrange raspberries in centre. Whip cream and pipe 8–10 rosettes around the edge. Top each with a sprig of mint.

Serves 8–10.

ICE-BOX CHEESECAKE

90 g (3 oz/⅓ cup) butter

185 g (6 oz/1⅔ cups) plain biscuit crumbs

½ teaspoon ground ginger

FILLING:

500 g (1 lb) full fat soft cheese

grated peel and juice of 1 lemon

4 eggs, separated

125 g (4 oz/½ cup) caster sugar

4 teaspoons powdered gelatine

315 ml (10 fl oz/1¼ cups) whipping cream

TO DECORATE:

440 g (14 oz) can pineapple rings

220 g (7 oz) red cherries

angelica 'leaves'

Grease and line a 20 cm (8 in) round, loose-bottomed cake tin. In a saucepan, melt butter, then stir in crumbs and ginger. Mix well, then press into base of cake tin.

In a bowl, beat cheese, lemon peel and juice, egg yolks and 60 g (2 oz/¼ cup) caster sugar until smooth.

Sprinkle gelatine over 2 table-spoons water in a small bowl and leave to soften for 2–3 minutes. Stand the bowl in a saucepan of hot water and stir until dissolved and quite hot. Stir into cheese mixture.

Loosely whip cream in a bowl and fold into cheese mixture with a large metal spoon. In a separate bowl, whisk egg whites with remaining sugar until firm, then fold into mixture. Pour onto biscuit base and freeze in ice compartment for 4 hours.

To decorate, cut pineapple rings in half and arrange them around the edge of the cheesecake. Place a cherry and 2 angelica 'leaves' in the centre of every other ring.

Serves 8–10.

Note: This cheesecake can be served straight from the refrigerator.

RASPBERRY CHEESE ROLL

4 eggs

125 g (4 oz/½ cup) caster sugar

60 g (2 oz/½ cup) ground almonds

6 teaspoons plain flour

FILLING:

185 g (6 oz) full fat soft cheese

155 ml (5 fl oz/⅔ cup) whipping cream

3 teaspoons icing sugar

500 g (1 lb) raspberries

TO DECORATE:

155 ml (5 fl oz/⅔ cup) whipping cream

6–8 sprigs of mint

Preheat oven to 200C (400F/Gas 6). Grease and line a 32.5 x 22.5 cm (13 x 9 in) baking sheet. Using a rotary or hand-held whisk, beat eggs and sugar in a bowl until mixture is thick enough to hold trail of the whisk when beaters are lifted.

Sift ground almonds and flour over egg mixture and fold in with a large metal spoon. Spread out sponge mixture on the baking sheet and bake in the oven for 10–12 minutes or until springy to the touch. Turn out onto a wire rack and leave to cool.

Put cheese into a blender or food processor with cream and icing sugar and blend until smooth – do not overblend or cream will separate.

Peel greaseproof paper off sponge and spread cheese mixture over sponge. Scatter three-quarters of the raspberries over top, then roll up lightly.

To decorate, whip cream and pipe a row of rosettes along top of the cheese roll. Decorate with remaining raspberries and sprigs of mint.

Serves 6–8.

APRICOT CHEESECAKE

90 g (3 oz/⅓ cup) butter
185 g (6 oz/1⅔ cups) digestive biscuit crumbs
FILLING:
250 g (8 oz) low fat soft cheese
155 ml (5 fl oz/⅔ cup) natural yogurt
90 g (3 oz/¾ cup) ground almonds
125 g (4 oz/½ cup) caster sugar
155 ml (5 fl oz/⅔ cup) whipping cream
3 teaspoons powdered gelatine
2 eggs
few drops almond essence
TO DECORATE:
440 g (14 oz) can apricot halves
155 ml (5 fl oz/⅔ cup) whipping cream

Grease and line a 20 cm (8 in) square cake tin. In a saucepan, melt butter, then stir in biscuit crumbs. Mix well, then press into base of cake tin.

In a bowl, beat cheese, yogurt, ground almonds and 60 g (2 oz/¼ cup) sugar until smooth. Loosely whip cream in a separate bowl, then fold into cheese mixture.

Sprinkle gelatine over 2 tablespoons water in a small bowl and leave to soften for 2–3 minutes. Stand the bowl in a saucepan of hot water and stir until dissolved and quite hot. Stir into cheese mixture.

Using a rotary or hand-held whisk, beat eggs, almond essence and remaining sugar in a bowl until mixture is thick enough to hold trail of the whisk when beaters are lifted. Fold beaten eggs into cheese mixture and pour onto biscuit base. Leave to set in the refrigerator for 2–3 hours.

To decorate, cut cheesecake into sixteen 5 cm (2 in) squares. Drain apricot halves and place one in centre of each square. Whip the cream and pipe a border of cream around edge of each square.

Serves 16.

BLUEBERRY CHEESECAKE

60 g (2 oz/½ cup) butter
125 g (4 oz/1½ cups) digestive or other semi-sweet biscuit crumbs
6 teaspoons sweet sherry
FILLING:
375 g (12 oz) Ricotta cheese
155 ml (5 fl oz/⅓ cup) natural yogurt
90 g (3 oz/⅓ cup) sugar
3 teaspoons lemon juice
2 eggs, separated
500 g (1 lb) blueberries
3 teaspoons powdered gelatine
TOPPING:
90 g (3 oz/¼ cup) redcurrant jelly
TO SERVE:
sprigs of mint
155 ml (5 fl oz/⅔ cup) whipping cream

Grease a 22.5 cm (9 in) round, loose-bottomed cake tin. In a saucepan, melt butter, then stir in biscuit crumbs and sherry. Mix well, then press into base of cake tin. Leave to firm in the refrigerator.

In a bowl, beat cheese, yogurt, 60 g (2 oz/¼ cup) sugar, lemon juice and egg yolks. Gently stir in 125 g (4 oz) of the blueberries.

Sprinkle gelatine over 2 tablespoons water in a small bowl and leave to soften for 2–3 minutes. Stand the bowl in a saucepan of hot water and stir until dissolved and quite hot. Stir into cheese.

Whisk egg whites with remaining sugar until firm and smooth. Fold into cheese mixture with a large metal spoon, then spoon onto biscuit base. Leave to set in refrigerator for 2–3 hours.

To make topping, melt redcurrant jelly in a small saucepan without boiling. Stir in remaining blueberries. Mix well, spread over cheesecake and chill. Decorate with mint and serve with whipped cream.

Serves 8–10.

COEURS À LA CRÈME

1.8 litres (3 pints/7 cups) milk
155 ml (5 fl oz/⅔ cup) whipping cream
1½ teaspoons rennet
TO DECORATE:
155 ml (5 fl oz/⅔ cup) whipping cream, if desired
250 g (8 oz) strawberries

Line 6 coeur à la crème moulds with a double layer of muslin. Put milk and cream into a saucepan and warm to blood temperature (do not allow to become too hot or the milk will not curdle properly). Stir in rennet and leave for 1 hour.

When the milk has curdled, pour contents of saucepan into a jelly bag suspended over an upturned kitchen stool. Place a bowl underneath to collect the whey. Leave to drain for about 50 minutes.

Empty contents of jelly bag into a glass bowl and stir curds until smooth. Divide cheese between moulds and leave in the refrigerator until firm.

Turn out onto individual serving plates. To decorate if desired, whip cream, then pipe onto moulds. Decorate with strawberry slices.

Serves 6.

REFRIGERATOR CHEESECAKE

90 g (3 oz/⅓ cup) butter
185 g (6 oz/1⅓ cups) semi-sweet biscuit crumbs
FILLING:
375 g (12 oz) full fat soft cheese
155 ml (5 fl oz/⅔ cup) thick sour cream
155 ml (5 fl oz/⅔ cup) natural yogurt
90 g (3 oz/⅓ cup) caster sugar
3 eggs, separated
4 teaspoons powdered gelatine
155 ml (5 fl oz/⅔ cup) whipping cream
TOPPING:
500 g (1 lb) assorted fresh fruits
30 g (1 oz) packet plain flan (cake) glaze, if desired

Grease and line a 20 cm (8 in) round, loose-bottomed cake tin. In a saucepan, melt butter, then stir in biscuit crumbs. Mix well, then press into base of cake tin.

In a bowl, beat cheese, sour cream, yogurt, 30 g (1 oz/5 teaspoons) caster sugar and egg yolks until smooth.

Sprinkle gelatine over 2 tablespoons water in a small bowl and leave to soften for 2–3 minutes. Stand the bowl in a saucepan of hot water and stir until dissolved and quite hot. Stir into cheese.

Loosely whip cream in a bowl and fold into cheese. Whisk egg whites with remaining sugar until firm, then fold into cheese. Turn into cake tin and leave to set in the refrigerator for 2–3 hours.

To decorate, cut fruits into even-sized pieces and arrange over top of cheesecake. Make up flan glaze according to packet instructions and brush over the fruit if desired.

Serves 8–10.

STRAWBERRY CHEESECAKES

60 g (2 oz/¼ cup) butter	
125 g (4 oz/1¼ cups) digestive biscuit crumbs	
FILLING:	
250 g (8 oz) full fat soft cheese	
315 ml (10 fl oz/1¼ cups) Greek style yogurt	
2 egg yolks	
90 g (3 oz/⅓ cup) caster sugar	
3 teaspoons powdered gelatine	
TOPPING:	
500 g (1 lb) strawberries	
155 ml (5 fl oz/⅔ cup) whipping cream	
8 sprigs of mint	

Place eight 8 cm (3½ in) muffin rings on a baking sheet and line with greaseproof paper. In a saucepan, melt butter, then stir in biscuit crumbs. Mix well, press into bottom of each ring, dividing mixture equally between them.

In a bowl, beat cheese and yogurt. Add egg yolks and sugar and beat until smooth.

Sprinkle gelatine over 2 tablespoons water in a small bowl and leave to soften for 2–3 minutes. Stand the bowl in a saucepan of hot water and stir until dissolved and quite hot. Stir into cheese mixture. Pour into muffin rings and leave to set in the refrigerator for 2–3 hours.

To decorate, slice strawberries and arrange over the cheesecakes. Whip cream and pipe a rosette of cream onto each cheesecake. Top each one with a sprig of mint.

Serves 8.

PEACH RASPBERRY CHEESECAKE

90 g (3 oz/⅓ cup) butter	
155 g (5 oz/1⅓ cups) ginger biscuit crumbs	
FILLING:	
125 g (4 oz) full fat soft cheese	
125 ml (4 fl oz/½ cup) Greek style yogurt	
90 g (3 oz/⅓ cup) caster sugar	
155 ml (5 fl oz/⅔ cup) whipping cream	
4 teaspoons powdered gelatine	
440 g (14 oz) can sliced peaches, roughly chopped	
2 eggs	
TO DECORATE:	
375 g (12 oz) raspberries	
155 ml (5 fl oz/⅔ cup) whipping cream	
30 g (1 oz) toasted flaked almonds	

Grease and line a 22.5 cm (9 in) round, loose-bottomed cake tin. In a saucepan, melt butter, then stir in biscuit crumbs. Mix well, then press into cake tin.

In a bowl, beat cheese, yogurt and 30 g (1 oz/5 teaspoons) sugar. Whip cream in a separate bowl and fold into cheese mixture.

Sprinkle gelatine over 2 tablespoons water in a small bowl and leave to soften for 2–3 minutes. Stand the bowl in a saucepan of hot water and stir until dissolved and quite hot. Stir into cheese mixture, then stir in chopped peaches.

Using a rotary or hand-held whisk, beat eggs and remaining sugar in a bowl until mixture is thick enough to hold trail of the whisk when beaters are lifted. Fold into cheese mixture. Turn into cake tin and leave to set in the refrigerator for 2–3 hours.

To decorate, arrange raspberries over surface, leaving a 2.5 cm (1 in) border around the edge. In a bowl, whip cream and pipe rosettes on the uncovered border. Decorate each rosette with 2 flaked almonds.

Serves 10.

ORANGE CHEESECAKE

90 g (3 oz/⅓ cup) butter
125 g (4 oz) round baby's rusks, crushed
60 g (2 oz/¼ cup) caster sugar
FILLING:
750 g (1½ lb) medium fat curd cheese
finely grated peel and juice of 1 orange
2 eggs
60 g (2 oz/¼ cup) caster sugar
TOPPING:
440 g (14 oz) can mandarin orange segments
30 g (1 oz) packet orange flan (cake) glaze
mint leaves

Preheat oven to 190C (375F/Gas 5). Grease and line a 22.5 cm (9 in) round, loose-bottomed cake tin. In a saucepan, melt butter, then stir in rusks and sugar. Mix well, then press into base and up sides of cake tin.

In a bowl, beat cheese, orange peel and juice, eggs and sugar until smooth. Turn into cake tin and bake in the oven for 40 minutes. Leave to cool before removing from tin.

To decorate, drain mandarin oranges on absorbent kitchen paper, then arrange on the top of cheesecake.

Make up flan glaze according to packet instructions and brush over mandarin oranges. Decorate each orange with a mint leaf.

Serves 8–10.

GOOSEBERRY CHEESECAKE

90 g (3 oz/⅓ cup) butter
125 g (4 oz/1¼ cups) digestive biscuit crumbs
30 g (1 oz/3 tablespoons) sunflower seeds
FILLING:
750 g (1½ lb) medium fat curd cheese
juice of 1 lemon
1 teaspoon orange flower water
2 eggs
60 g (2 oz/¼ cup) caster sugar
TOPPING:
440 g (14 oz) can gooseberries
6 teaspoons cornflour
TO SERVE:
cream or yogurt

Preheat oven to 190C (375F/Gas 5). Grease and line a 22.5 cm (9 in) round, loose-bottomed cake tin. In a saucepan, melt butter, then stir in biscuit crumbs and sunflower seeds. Mix well, then press into cake tin.

In a bowl, beat cheese, lemon juice, orange flower water, eggs and sugar. Turn into cake tin and bake in the oven for 40 minutes. Leave to cool.

Meanwhile, make topping. Drain gooseberries and put juice into a small saucepan. Bring to the boil. Mix cornflour with 4 tablespoons water. Stir into gooseberry juice and simmer to thicken. Add gooseberries, stir gently, then spread over cheesecake.

When cheesecake is cold, remove from tin and serve with cream or yogurt.

Serves 8–10.

REDCURRANT CHEESECAKE

60 g (2 oz/¼ cup) butter
125 g (4 oz/1¼ cups) digestive biscuit crumbs
FILLING:
750 g (1½ lb) medium fat curd cheese
finely grated peel and juice of 1 lemon
2 eggs
60 g (2 oz/¼ cup) caster sugar
375 g (12 oz) redcurrants, thawed if frozen
TOPPING:
90 g (3 oz/¼ cup) redcurrant jelly
8–10 sprigs of mint

Preheat oven to 190C (375F/Gas 5). Grease and line a 22.5 cm (9 in) round, loose-bottomed cake tin. In a saucepan, melt butter, then stir in biscuit crumbs. Mix well, then press into cake tin.

In a bowl, beat cheese, lemon peel and juice, eggs and sugar. Stir 125 g (4 oz) of the redcurrants into cheese mixture. Turn into cake tin and bake in the oven for 45 minutes.

To make topping, melt redcurrant jelly in a saucepan. Stir in remaining redcurrants and spread over surface of cheesecake. Leave to cool before removing from tin. Decorate with sprigs of mint.

Serves 8–10.

LIQUEUR CHEESECAKE

90 g (3 oz/⅓ cup) butter
185 g (6 oz/1⅔ cups) digestive biscuit crumbs
FILLING:
500 g (1 lb) Ricotta cheese
155 ml (5 fl oz/⅔ cup) thick sour cream
3 eggs
3 teaspoons plain flour
90 g (3 oz/⅓ cup) soft brown sugar
finely grated peel and juice of 2 oranges
75 ml (2½ fl oz/⅓ cup) Grand Marnier
TO DECORATE:
3 small oranges
155 ml (5 fl oz/⅔ cup) whipping cream
250 g (8 oz) strawberries

Preheat oven to 180C (350F/Gas 4). Grease and line a 22.5 cm (9 in) round, spring-form cake tin. In a saucepan, melt butter, then stir in biscuit crumbs. Mix well, then press into base of cake tin.

In a bowl, beat cheese, sour cream, eggs, flour and sugar. Add orange peel and juice and Grand Marnier and beat until smooth. Turn into cake tin and bake in the oven for 50 minutes. Leave to cool before removing from the tin.

To decorate, cut oranges into 0.5 cm (¼ in) slices. Make a cut from centre to edge of each slice, then hold slice at each side of cut and twist to form an S shape. Arrange orange twists around edge of cheesecake.

Whip cream in a bowl, then pipe a rosette of cream into each orange twist and add a strawberry.

Serves 8–10.

CAMPARI CHEESECAKE

90 g (3 oz/⅓ cup) butter
185 g (6 oz/1⅔ cups) plain biscuit crumbs
FILLING:
250 g (8 oz) low fat soft cheese
155 ml (5 fl oz/⅔ cup) natural yogurt
155 ml (5 fl oz/⅔ cup) whipping cream
finely grated peel and juice of 1 pink grapefruit
75 ml (2½ fl oz/⅓ cup) Campari
4 teaspoons powdered gelatine
2 eggs
60 g (2 oz/¼ cup) caster sugar
TO DECORATE:
2 kiwi fruit
2 pink grapefruit, peeled and divided into segments
5 maraschino cherries, halved

Grease and line a 20 cm (8 in) round, loose-bottomed cake tin. In a saucepan, melt butter, then stir in biscuit crumbs. Mix well, then press into base of cake tin.

In a bowl, beat cheese, yogurt and cream until smooth. Add grapefruit peel and juice and Campari and beat until smooth.

Sprinkle gelatine over 2 tablespoons water in a small bowl and leave to soften for 2–3 minutes. Stand bowl in a saucepan of hot water and stir until dissolved. Stir into cheese mixture.

Using a rotary or hand-held whisk, beat eggs and sugar in a bowl until mixture is thick enough to hold trail of the whisk when beaters are lifted. Fold beaten eggs into cheese mixture, then turn into cake tin. Leave to set in the refrigerator for 2–3 hours.

To decorate, slice kiwi fruit. Turn out cheesecake and arrange segments of grapefruit, slices of kiwi fruit and maraschino cherries around the edge.

Serves 8–10.

TIPSY CHEESECAKE

90 g (3 oz/⅓ cup) butter
185 g (6 oz/1⅔ cups) plain biscuit crumbs
FILLING:
60 g (2 oz) macaroons
75 ml (2½ fl oz/⅓ cup) dry sherry
375 g (12 oz) medium fat curd cheese
155 ml (5 fl oz/⅔ cup) whipping cream
2 eggs
90 g (3 oz/⅓ cup) caster sugar
500 g (1 lb) raspberries
30 g (1 oz/2 tablespoons) icing sugar

Put the macaroons for the filling into a small bowl. Pour over the sherry and leave to soak for 15–20 minutes until sherry is absorbed.

Meanwhile, preheat oven to 180C (350F/Gas 4). Grease and line a 20 cm (8 in) round, loose-bottomed cake tin. In a saucepan, melt butter, then stir in biscuit crumbs. Mix well, then press into base of cake tin.

In a bowl, beat cheese, cream, eggs and caster sugar until smooth (do not overbeat or cheesecake will rise too much during baking).

Stir macaroons into mixture, trying not to break them up. Stir in 185 g (6 oz) of the raspberries. Turn into cake tin and bake in the oven for 50 minutes. Leave to cool before removing from tin.

To decorate, dust surface of cheesecake with icing sugar and arrange remaining raspberries around edge in 3 rows.

Serves 6–8.

WHITE CHOCOLATE CAKE

60 g (2 oz/¼ cup) butter
125 g (4 oz/1¼ cups) chocolate digestive biscuit crumbs
FILLING:
375 g (12 oz) Ricotta cheese
185 g (6 oz/1 cup) sweet chestnut purée
155 ml (5 fl oz/⅔ cup) whipping cream
125 g (4 oz) white chocolate, broken into pieces
6 teaspoons cognac
3 eggs
3 teaspoons plain flour
TO DECORATE:
125 g (4 oz) white chocolate
155 ml (5 fl oz/⅔ cup) whipping cream
10 pieces candied chestnut
caster sugar
10 angelica 'leaves'

Preheat oven to 180C (350F/Gas 4). Grease and line a 20 cm (8 in) round, loose-bottomed cake tin. In a saucepan, melt butter, then stir in biscuit crumbs. Mix well and press into base of cake tin.

In a bowl, beat cheese and chestnut purée. Bring cream to the boil in a small saucepan. Remove from heat, add chocolate and stir until melted. Add cognac and stir into cheese mixture. Add eggs and flour and beat well. Turn into cake tin and bake in the oven for 1 hour. Leave to cool before removing from tin.

To decorate, grate white chocolate over surface of cheesecake. Whip cream and pipe a border of 10 large rosettes around edge and decorate with pieces of candied chestnut rolled in caster sugar and topped with angelica 'leaves'.

Serves 10–12.

CHOC & WHISKY CHEESECAKE

60 g (2 oz/¼ cup) butter
185 g (6 oz/1⅔ cups) ginger biscuit crumbs
FILLING:
750 g (1½ lb) full fat soft cheese
60 g (2 oz/¼ cup) soft brown sugar
2 eggs
6 teaspoons cocoa powder
2 teaspoons ground ginger
155 ml (5 fl oz/⅔ cup) whipping cream
250 g (8 oz) plain (dark) chocolate, broken into pieces
90 ml (3 fl oz/⅓ cup) whisky
TO DECORATE:
6 teaspoons cocoa powder
4 teaspoons icing sugar
½ teaspoon ground ginger

Preheat oven to 180C (350F/Gas 4). Grease and line a 20 cm (8 in) round, loose-bottomed cake tin. In a saucepan, melt butter, then stir in biscuit crumbs. Mix well, then press into base of cake tin.

To make filling, beat together cheese, brown sugar and eggs in a bowl. Sift in cocoa powder and ginger and beat until smooth. Bring cream to boil in a small saucepan. Remove from heat, add chocolate and stir until melted. Stir in whisky and blend into cheese mixture.

Turn into cake tin and bake in the oven for 45 minutes. Leave to cool before removing from cake tin.

To decorate, cut out 5 strips of greaseproof paper 2 cm (¾ in) wide and lay them at intervals over surface of cheesecake. Mix together cocoa powder, icing sugar and ground ginger, then sift over cake. Carefully remove strips and serve at once.

Serves 8–10.

RICH CHOCOLATE CHEESECAKE

90 g (3 oz/⅓ cup) butter
185 g (6 oz/1⅔ cups) chocolate digestive biscuit crumbs
FILLING:
750 g (1½ lb) full fat soft cheese
3 eggs
60 g (2 oz/¼ cup) dark soft brown sugar
3 tablespoons molasses or black treacle
6 teaspoons cocoa powder
1 teaspoon ground allspice
finely grated peel and juice of 1 orange
155 ml (5 fl oz/⅔ cup) whipping cream
250 g (8 oz) plain (dark) chocolate, broken into pieces
60 g (2 oz/¼ cup) soft unsalted butter
TOPPING:
250 g (8 oz) plain (dark) chocolate, flaked
125 g (4 oz) white chocolate, flaked

Preheat oven to 180C (350F/Gas 4). Grease and line a 22.5 cm (9 in) round, loose-bottomed cake tin. In a saucepan, melt butter, then stir in crumbs. Mix, then press into tin.

In a bowl, beat cheese, eggs, sugar, molasses or black treacle, cocoa powder, allspice, orange peel and juice. Bring cream to the boil in a small saucepan. Remove from the heat, add chocolate and stir until melted. Beat in butter, then blend into cheese mixture.

Turn into cake tin and bake in the oven for 50 minutes. Leave to cool before removing from tin.

To decorate, arrange plain (dark) chocolate flakes in overlapping layers around edge of cake, alternating with the 2 coloured chocolates towards the centre.

Serves 10–12.

LEMON MERINGUE POSSET

125 g (4 oz/½ cup) butter
250 g (8 oz/2¼ cups) digestive biscuit crumbs
FILLING:
3 egg yolks
470 ml (15 fl oz/1¾ cups) double (heavy) cream
juice of 2 lemons
90 g (3 oz/⅓ cup) caster sugar
TOPPING:
3 egg whites
30 g (1 oz/5 teaspoons) caster sugar, plus extra for sprinkling
lemon twist and sprig of mint

Grease and line a 20 cm (8 in) flan tin. In a saucepan, melt butter, then stir in biscuit crumbs. Mix well, then press into base and up sides of flan tin.

In a bowl, whisk egg yolks until pale in colour. Bring cream to the boil in a saucepan. Add lemon juice and sugar. Whisk into egg yolks, then spoon onto biscuit base. Leave to set in the refrigerator for 2–3 hours.

To make topping, whisk egg whites in a bowl with 30 g (1 oz/5 teaspoons) sugar until stiff, then pile onto the flan. Sprinkle with sugar and brown under a hot grill. Decorate with mint and lemon twist.

Serves 8–10.

INDEX